THE
EUCHARIST
AND HUMAN
LIBERATION

THE
EUCHARIST
AND HUMAN
LIBERATION

Tissa Balasuriya, O.M.I.

ORBIS BOOKS

Maryknoll, New York 10545

1979

Library of Congress Cataloging in Publication Data

Balasuriya, Tissa.
  The Eucharist and human liberation.

  1. Lord's Supper—Catholic Church. I. Title.
BX2215.2.B33   234'.163   78-9160
ISBN 0-88344-118-7

The Catholic Foreign Mission Society of America (Maryknoll) recruits and trains people for overseas missionary service. Through Orbis Books Maryknoll aims to foster the international dialogue that is essential to mission. The books published, however, reflect the opinions of their authors and are not meant to represent the official position of the Society.

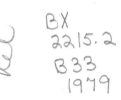
The church should light the sacred candle of the resurrection not merely through its preaching within its walls, but also through actions outside the walls of the church.

We should dedicate ourselves to the task of reviving conscience and justice, which will bless us with a brighter and more just society.

Cardinal Stephen Kim Su-Whan of Korea

CONTENTS

Foreword

It is with a certain sense of pride that I introduce this book of Father Balasuriya to the general public.

I have always bemoaned the fact that Asia after so many years of Christianity has not produced any significant theological writing. This book can, without exaggeration, be said to contain the theological reflections of an Asian theologian. It is a faith reflection of a priest, on one of the most sacred and essential functions of the priest—the celebration of the Eucharist.

The Asian faith experience is a unique and a complex one—different from the Latin American or the African experience, though there may be some elements in common. The author tries to make articulate this experience out of a sheer loyalty to the Universal Church.

He tries to portray to us what the Eucharist should be in the light of Scripture and tradition. He therefore takes a close look at what it has been until now and argues that this most liberative act has been so domesticated by a socio-economic system that it now enslaves and domesticates its participants.

He is also extremely sensitive to the longings and searchings of committed priests to make the Eucharist meaningful to themselves and to society.

He writes with a deep concern for and a love of the priesthood and the Eucharist, while at the same time calling for new thinking on the meaning of these realities today.

Leo Nanayakkara, O.S.B.
Bishop of Badulla, Sri Lanka

Preface

The Eucharist presents us with a paradox. Jesus gave a challenging spiritual meaning to the festive meal of the Jews commemorating their liberation from slavery in Egypt. In bequeathing this to the community of his followers, Jesus manifested his genius as a spiritual leader of humanity. For two thousand years the churches have continued to celebrate the Eucharist in his memory. The Eucharist has been, and is, offered under diverse situations. Hundreds of millions all over the world meet every Sunday, year after year. Millions of men, women, and children have drawn personal inspiration through the centuries from the Eucharist and from prayer to Jesus present in the tabernacles the world over.

On the other hand, Christians have divided themselves into different sects partly on their views concerning the Eucharist. Wars of religion have marred the history of the followers of Jesus. But even more tragic is the way in which the Eucharist has been domesticated within the dominant social establishments of the day. Its radical demands have been largely neutralized. Its cutting edge has been blunted. Worse still, it has been and is being used as a legitimation of cruel exploitation. Many have given up frequenting the Sunday Eucharist, especially in the western countries. The working classes feel alienated from it and by it.

An agonizing question presents itself to our minds. Why is it that in spite of hundreds of thousands of eucharistic celebrations, Christians continue as selfish as before? Why have the "Christian" peoples been the most cruel colonizers of human history? Why is the gap of income, wealth, knowledge, and power growing in the world today—and

that in favor of the "Christian" peoples? Why is it that
persons and people who proclaim eucharistic love and
sharing deprive the poor people of the world of food, capi-
tal, employment, and even land? Why do they prefer
cigarettes and liquor to food and drink for the one-third of
humanity that goes hungry to bed each night? Why are
cars, cosmetics, pet dogs, horses, and bombs preferred to
human children? Why mass human sterilization in poor
countries and affluence unto disease and pollution of nature among the rich?

Father Peter Pillai, an ardent apostle of social justice in
Sri Lanka, often mentioned with a sense of uneasiness
that in Sri Lanka some of the worst slums are in areas
inhabited by Catholics. He spoke of Mutwal in Colombo and
Munnakkara in Negombo. Here tens of thousands live in
terrible squalor and misery in the shadow of monumental
churches. Over one hundred thousand Masses have been
celebrated in these places over the decades. Yet inequalities grow. The rich live comfortably like Dives in the
Gospel story. The poor eke out a miserable existence in
their hovels. And now the luxurious tourist hotels add
further contrasts to this sorrowful environment.

The churches have spoken during the last two decades of
identification with the poor, but how minimal have been
the changes in the churches as a whole! All the same, the
deep social commitment of some Christian groups is often
inspired by a more meaningful celebration of the Eucharist. This is generally in small groups, among youth, workers, women, religious, priests, and the like. They are, not
infrequently, marginalized by the official church authorities. Eucharistic life pulsates among them. But the
official church authorities tend to look askance at them,
consider them "rebels" and, in any case, persons who do
not know or value the "spiritual life." One asks, has the
dynamism flowing from the Lord's Supper and his final
sacrifice been suffocated by ritual, formalism, and conformity to a prevailing power system? Yet, when well
celebrated we have a glimpse of the great potential for

human motivation in the Eucharist. This is a source of hope. The lethargy and nonchalance of the powerful official controllers of the eucharistic rites lead one to near despair concerning the possibility of the churches as a whole responding meaningfully to the demands of humanity. Yet are not the churches and religions one of the few hopes for the exploited poor of the world today?

This book tries to grapple with some of these sad paradoxes. It is meant to stimulate further reflection. Many of its sections need much further study and investigation. It is not presented as an exhaustive or all-inclusive work. Many concerns of traditional treatises on the Eucharist are not discussed here. This is an effort to contribute in some small way to the ongoing reflection on the Eucharist in relation to the life of human beings today. I hope it will help toward a better understanding of the spiritual life itself.

I will be glad to receive any comments. I would not be surprised if there are strong reactions to it. To some this book itself may seem a paradox! Perhaps it is through the agony of living these tensions and articulating them together that we can go toward a theology truer to Jesus and closer to the griefs and sorrows and the hopes and aspirations of the men, women, and children of our age.

Tissa Balasuriya, O.M.I.
Centre for Society and Religion
Colombo, Sri Lanka

Chapter I

Eucharist as Central to the Christian Community

"Do this in commemoration of me." Jesus gave this mandate to his apostles at the Last Supper. This was full of meaning. He was participating in a meal—the paschal meal. Through this he was sharing with them the secret of his life. He explained to them the cause for which he lived and struggled. The next forty-eight hours saw his arrest, trial, and crucifixion. He died because he stood firmly for integral human liberation and fulfillment. He courageously opposed every form of oppression and injustice. His obedience to God his Father was in this service to humanity. He wanted his followers to do likewise.

Ever since then the eucharistic meal has been a gathering that has characterized the followers of Jesus. Throughout the centuries believers of Christ have met to break bread and worship God in and through Jesus. They have done so under many different conditions. The Eucharist was offered in the catacombs of Rome when Christianity was persecuted. Later the Eucharist was the symbol of triumphant Christianity when it was celebrated at the high altar of the grand Roman basilicas. The monasteries were centers of eucharistic devotion in the feudal period. The modern period saw the expansion of Europe into its colonial empire. The Eucharist was taken to the corners of the earth by priests in combination with colonial rulers. The Catholic-Protestant divisions and even wars of religion had also a relation to their different understanding concerning the Eucharist. In more recent decades the eucharistic sacrifice has been offered in prisons in many countries, on the sea, and in the air. Hundreds of millions of believers meet every Sunday all over the world to "do this in commemoration of me."

Yet the understanding concerning the Eucharist has not always been the same throughout these centuries in the different lands and among conflicting social classes. In fact the meaning of the Eucharist has been altered by the social pressures. There have been serious distortions in its meaning. Whereas it began with the sacrifice of self for the liberation of others, it has for long been a means of enslavement and domestication of believers. The Eucharist has always remained central to Christianity; but it has been adjusted to suit the needs of the dominant groups in the churches. There has been *a social conditioning of the Eucharist*. This is only one aspect of the overall subordination of the Christian religion to the powers that be in society. We shall see this in our brief analysis of the cult of the Eucharist over the centuries. Feudalism, capitalism, colonialism, racism, and sexism have all tended to make the Eucharist conform to their values and priorities. The priesthood, which is considered the celebrant and guardian of the Eucharist, has also been thought of in terms of the needs of the social establishment of the day. The words of the Eucharist have been maintained but their meaning has been evacuated, substituted, or distorted. The extent to which even the core rites of a religion can thus be subjected to serve the ruling elites is not surprising but frightening.

It is not without significance that during many centuries the rite for the celebration of the Eucharist was maintained rigidly according to rules set down by the central authority in the church. Catholics meet generally around the Sunday Mass. The other sacraments—baptism, confirmation, penance, marriage, holy orders, and the last rites—have also a relationship to the Eucharist. Much of the time of the parish priests and

Christian communities is taken up with the sacraments, particularly the Sunday Mass.

The Mass has had, and still has to a large extent, a great measure of rigid uniformity: the same rites, readings predetermined for the whole year, the cycle of years. The same feasts repeat themselves in a cycle. Even the vestments, words, and gestures have been centrally controlled. Only the sermon brought in some spontaneity. But this too had its limits. The advocates of *sacramental unity* would find in this a wonderful witness to the oneness of the church. But it does also provide a very supple instrument for the domestication of the believers. The Mass adjusts itself very little even to major social revolutions or calamities. Generally the Christian community continues to worship as if nothing much has taken place over the centuries. The impression created is that here is an efficacious way of personal sanctification. For sanctity is regarded as an "otherwordly" reality. The ups and downs of life need not concern the "holy" person or the holiness of persons. The high and low in society can meet together, pray together, and go back to their different styles of life feeling comforted in the Mass.

While such uniformity has its values, it will be seen that it is also the guarantee of social conformism and conservatism among Christians. In their principal and perhaps only contact as a group, they perform rigid roles and go away without in any real way questioning themselves on the vital issues of the day. Naturally to raise such issues would be to divide the "Christian community." And since "unity" is presupposed to be a value, the real issues are sent under the beautiful carpet at the altar. So long as the "faithful" can be conditioned to accept this, the unity persists. But when the divisions become too sharp and unbearable, a break or rupture takes place.

The divisions in Christendom have also generally related to the Eucharist and the way it is celebrated. The Protestant Reformation in the sixteenth century was caused partly by the desire of the peoples of northern

Europe to get away from the ecclesiastical control of the southerners, especially the Latins. It had too a relation to the imperial expansion of different western peoples and the growth of commercial and later industrial capitalism. These could not be easily reconciled with the claims of Catholicism in teaching and in moral, economic, and political life—not to mention papal supremacy. The causes of division were of a socio-economic and political nature also; but the expressions of divergences in the theological sphere related closely to the Eucharist, the sacraments, the priesthood, sanctification, and redemption. This is understandable, for the Christians as religious communities met around the Eucharist under the leadership of the clergy. A new church would thus have to have a newness in the Eucharist too. Separation at the eucharistic table became symbolic of a wider separation in social, economic, political, and cultural life.

In the wars of religion, the Mass became central for the Catholics. Even today the Irish Catholics affirm "it is the Mass that matters." The Mass for them was a gathering and a ceremony that affirmed their difference from the ruling Protestant British. Under conditions of persecution and resistance to it, the Mass can acquire a particular power of keeping alive a flame of faith.

In the subsequent colonial expansion the missionaries transplanted the Eucharist according to their home models, especially after the Reformation. The conquered peoples were baptized where possible—if they had not already been exterminated. Through the baptisms, new churches were begun. New Christians were brought up in the tradition and according to the thinking of the Western European churches. The Eucharist was transplanted lock, stock, and barrel. European wine was imported, where necessary, in order to continue the same rite. The Christians were generally grouped together in separate areas or communities. The new communities met on Sundays for the Eucharist. It is significant that the colonizers and colonized, the exploiter and exploited could meet at the same "table," while the rape of these colonial countries was going on. Why was this possible? Was it because the exploited were converted to respect the rights of others? Or were the exploited conditioned, even ideologically, to accept foreign rule and domination? By and large it was the latter. The individual missionaries may have been zealous and kind, but the system they represented and collaborated with was brutal.

Christian theology has not yet reflected adequately on this *domestication of the sacraments within the colonial system*. It was not necessary for Europeans to react to this unfavorably. They were at the receiving end of benefits of the empire, and converts to Christianity meant supporters of the continuance of the empire. Western European workers reacted to the alliance of the clergy with their own capitalist class by keeping away from the Sunday Mass. Hence the phenomenon of the "dechristianization" of Europe in the nineteenth and twentieth centuries. But those who decided church policies in Europe were not workers. They were immune from the sufferings of the burden of imperialism. Hence they could not see how the Eucharist they brought to African, Asian, and Latin American countries was conditioned by their own needs and priorities.

It is extremely important that this problem be well understood by all. For there has been such an exceptional buildup of a sense of the spiritual around the Eucharist and the Mass that it is hardly possible to discuss these issues without being considered irreverent and almost outside the pale of Christianity. The aura of sanctity surrounding the rites of the Eucharist have made discussion extremely difficult. Yet if we take up these issues, it is not to belittle the sacrifice of Christ and our participation in it, but rather to try to give it a more real, deeper, and fuller meaning in our own circumstances. The "adaptation" of the Christian religion to Asian, African, and Latin American countries is not merely a matter of language, rites, music, art, or even of having native clergy and bishops. We have to go through a much deeper revaluation of the whole thought and value content of what passes for Christianity and faith.

We have to try to do so because Christianity itself has been distorted and deformed by its alliance with world domination. Those of us who have been at the receiving end of modern history know how Christianity has been thus siding with oppression. We have to reflect from the position of the oppressed. We have to ask ourselves how much the Eucharist helps in our liberation. The Eucharist was meant to be a symbol, a commemoration and a participation in Jesus' liberative action. But today, when it is allied to domination, its impact is toward preserving the status quo. Those who are oppressed as workers and marginalized groups in our own countries feel this even more; or at least suffer from it. The women, who are an oppressed half of humanity, are also made passive recipients at the Eucharist. An active role has been denied them during many centuries. Hence the oppressed peoples and groups have to ask: To what extent is our official worship in the churches a real means of objective liberation? Does it help transform persons genuinely to accept the eucharistic values of sharing? In that sense does it help build the kingdom of God objectively according to values of truth, love, justice, and peace?

It will be seen that these questions go far beyond what has been raised in the general works on liturgy, or even in Vatican Council II. Our concern is with a total reorientation of Christianity to become a liberating power and not an ally of oppression. We have to ask these questions precisely because the Eucharist is central to the Christian community. No serious internal change can come about in this community as such without the Sunday Eucharist itself being affected. On the other hand, if the message and manner of the eucharistic celebration remain implicitly status quo-oriented then the Christian community would not be relating to the needs and changes in society as a community.

In this connection and perspective we can understand the acute controversies that have raged in the Roman Catholic church during the past twenty years even concerning the eucharistic fast. The younger generation may not remember that till about two decades ago people had to abstain even from water from midnight of the previous day for celebrating Mass on the following morning. The controls were rigid and universal. Mass could be celebrated only in the morning. It was offered by individual priests alone, at an altar with the face of the priest turned away from the people, all in Latin, everywhere in the Roman Catholic church. All the details of the gestures of the Mass were preordained. In the 1950s theologians and young active Christian groups began to question this rigidity. Were all these rules necessary? Pope Pius XII relaxed the rule of fasting by permitting the drinking of water before receiving Communion. These changes were further extended to the present rather liberal position.

It is noteworthy that there were major debates around almost each minor issue. Thus in most Catholic countries heated exchanges of views have taken place concerning the change in the position of the altar, the gestures of the celebrant at Mass, the language of the readings, the language of the canon, the texts of the readings, the translations, the type of music, the words of the songs or hymns, the musical instruments to be used, the posture of the laity, the mode of receiving Communion (in the hand or on the tongue), receiving under both kinds (bread and wine), the type of bread or host, the possibilities of concelebration, evening Masses, wedding Masses in the evening, Masses in the home, group Masses, the need of vestments and their type, the role of women in the liturgy. Many of these issues have been resolved in the course of two decades in favor of changes. The conflicts are now being forgotten except by a few older persons who may want the old Latin Mass. The fact that churchgoing Catholics were divided over such minor issues and even concentrated on them for fifteen or twenty years is significant. The overall fundamental questions and changes in society seemed less relevant to the worshiping community. This shows how difficult it was for a rigidly conservative religious group to get away from its conditioning and navel-gazing postures. The pope in Rome had to be consulted for the resolution of these issues!

Yet we should see clearly that all these changes are marginal to the main problem that the whole Mass is still a bulwark of social conservatism and not yet a means of human liberation. It is useful that rubricists, members of liturgical commissions, seminary personnel, lay activists, episcopal commissions, Catholic journalists, and many persons "holily" enraged about the changes realize what minor and external aspects of the liturgy they have been dealing with and quarreling about during fifteen or twenty of the most eventful years in history. We need a bit of a sense of humor to be able to laugh at ourselves. To what pettinesses we have been confining so much of our attention!

The deeper dimension of the Eucharist will not come merely from the books of liturgy. Even if we trace our sources for a thousand years we may not find the liberative dimension of the Eucharist. The Eucharist has been a victim of the social forces for an even longer period. It is a theology that goes back to the original sources of the Christian religion and relates to today's real issues that can help in the effective revitalization of the liturgy.

In the meantime, the groups more actively committed to human liberation and the values of the kingdom of God tend to move away from too rigid a liturgy in which there is no spontaneity and authenticity. They have small group Masses or paraliturgies that can relate better to their needs, struggles, and tensions as well as to the problems of the people as a whole. The Catholic church will have to be really attentive to this question if it does not wish to see a much larger alienation of people from its Sunday cultic gathering. Already in Europe the Sunday Mass attracts very few people. The trends in the Americas are in the same direction, except where significant changes have taken place. Not even the orientations of Vatican II are adequate to meet these issues genuinely. Vatican II did not have a clear analysis of the domestication of the liturgy by the power elites in Europe and elsewhere. It gave certain guidelines for renewal and left effective power in the hands of the bishops, episcopal commissions, and the Roman curia.

In order that we may participate creatively in the process of relating the Eucharist to personal and societal liberation, it is necessary that we have a better understanding of the Eucharist in its sources, its history, and in contemporary society. This small book tries to provide a basis for such a discussion and reflection. We are aware of its many limitations. It presents a study from a point of view that many may not agree with. Some may be shocked by its conclusions or implications. I hope this will not prevent anyone from seeing the basic purpose, namely, for believers to realize more clearly and deeply the meaning of Jesus Christ and of participating in his life and liberative action for the benefit of all humankind.

This is my commandment, that you love one another as I have loved you. Greater love than this no one has, that one lays down his life for his friends. You are my friends if you do the things I command you (John 15:12–14).

Chapter II

The Old Testament Background

Jesus instituted the Eucharist on the night of the Jewish Pasch. It was the national feast, a celebration of their independence, their liberation from slavery in Egypt. Jesus gave a new, deeper, and more universal meaning to this event.

In order to understand the Eucharist it is therefore necessary to reflect on the events that the Jewish paschal meal commemorated. The Jews went to Egypt after Joseph, the son of Jacob, had found favor with the Pharaoh. But years after, they had lost favor with the rulers. *They were oppressed by Egyptians.* Exodus describes their flight. The Egyptians were shrewd exploiters. "They set task masters over the Jews to afflict them with heavy burdens" (Exod. 8:11). And the Egyptians were in dread of the people of Israel. "So they made the people of Israel serve with rigor, and made their lives bitter with hard service, in mortar and brick, and in all kinds of work in the field" (1:13).

Yet, "the more they were oppressed, the more they multiplied and the more they spread abroad." Pharaoh then asked the midwives to kill the male children of the Jews at birth—to prevent males being a threat to the exploiting masters. The midwives conscientiously disobeyed and the Israelites multiplied.

"The people of Israel groaned under their bondage . . . and their cry came up to God. And God heard their groaning, and God remembered his covenant with Abraham, with Isaac, and with Jacob. And God saw the people of Israel, and God knew their condition" (Exod. 2:23–25).

10

GOD'S COVENANT

God called Moses to lead them out of slavery. "I have seen the affliction of my people ... and I have come down to deliver them out of the hand of the Egyptians, and to bring them up out of that land to a good and broad land, a land flowing with milk and honey." The liberation which God wrought for his people was a *political liberation*. God bears witness here to the need of political action, as liberation was impossible otherwise.

Liberation for the Jews was then not a matter of social service, or of welfare gifts from the cruel pharaoh and the oppressive Egyptians. It was not an issue of mere productivity. Pharaoh and the exploiters accused their slaves of being lazy and increased their work load. The Israelites helped build imposing monuments to the pharaohs, but for 430 years they remained enslaved. Exploitation became worse. The firstborn of the Israelites had to be killed. (How like some family-planning policies sponsored by the selfish rich today.)

God's option was not merely political, it was violent. Only a revolutionary breakaway from slavery would take his chosen people onto the road to freedom and a more just society. *Moses and Aaron were violent revolutionary leaders.* God told them: "I know that the king of Egypt will not let you go unless compelled by a mighty hand. So I will stretch out my hand and smite Egypt.... After that he will let you go" (Exod. 3:19–20). The Jews were reluctant to undertake this struggle. They grumbled before it and during the long march through the desert.

Manna and quail were provided by God as food for the Jews on the march. It was God's sustenance of his people in their long and bitter trek away from a condition of structural exploitation and alienation. They could not conserve the manna for the following day, except for the Sabbath. They received just what was required. It was an egalitarian gift. They had to go through the desert in faith. They had to endure untold hardships in the hope of arriving in the promised land.

God was thus deeply engaged in the history of his people. Their freedom from a sinful situation was his concern. His kingdom was not outside history, not unrelated to their anguish and their struggles. The people had to participate in this heroic effort. They could not liberate themselves with mere goodwill, prayer, or persuasion. They had to fight their way to the promised Jerusalem.

The liberation of the Jews from Egypt prefigures the subsequent liberation of the whole of humankind in Christ. The paschal feast of the Christians harks back to this central event of the Old Testament, which was the pledge of God's concern for his chosen people. It is very important for us to reflect that the core event of the history of Israel in the Old Testament was a political event.

The institution of the Eucharist is thus closely connected to the struggle of the Jewish people for their liberation.

GOD'S JUDGMENT ON IRRELEVANT SACRIFICES

The prophets were the great spiritual leaders of the people of Israel. They spoke a clear word from God. They gave a message to the people from their own historical situation. The prophets were quite categorical in their condemnation of mere empty ritual that had no relation to love and justice in real life. For them such a liturgical "worship" was a mockery of God and human beings insofar as there was no relation to God's commandment of faith in him and love of neighbor. The duties to God and neighbor were intimately linked. We see this in several prophets.

> What to me is the multitude of your sacrifices?
> says the Lord;
> I have had enough of burnt offerings of rams
> and the fat of fed beasts;
> I do not delight in the blood of bulls,
> or of lambs, or of he-goats.
> When you come to appear before me,
> who requires of you

this trampling of my courts?
Bring no more vain offerings;
incense is an abomination to me.
New moon and sabbath and the calling of assemblies—
I cannot endure iniquity and solemn assembly.
Your new moons and your appointed feasts
my soul hates;
they have become a burden to me,
I am weary of bearing them.
When you spread forth your hands
I will hide my eyes from you;
even though you make many prayers,
I will not listen;
your hands are full of blood.
Wash yourselves; make yourselves clean;
remove the evil of your doings
from before my eyes;
cease to do evil,
learn to do good;
seek justice,
correct oppression;
defend the fatherless,
plead for the widow (Isa. 1:11–17).

Fasting like yours this day will not make your voice to be heard
on high. . . . Is not this the sort of fast that pleases me? . . . to
break unjust fetters and undo the things of the yoke, to let the
oppressed go free and break every yoke; to share your bread with
the hungry and shelter the homeless poor; to clothe the man you
see to be naked and not turn from your own kin. Then will your
light shine like the dawn and your wound be quickly healed over
(Isa. 58:4–8).

I hate and despise your feasts. Let me have no more of the din of
your chanting, . . . but let justice flow like water and integrity
like an unfailing stream (Amos 5:21–24).

In the very small book of Micah, the word of the Lord is
clear against prayer and worship offered by evildoers.
Micah has a strong condemnation against the rulers of
Israel.

And I said: Hear, you heads of Jacob and rulers of the house of Israel! Is it not for you to know justice?—you who hate the good and love the evil, who tear the skin off from my people and their flesh from off their bones, who eat the flesh of my people and flay their skin from off them, and break their bones in pieces, and chop them up like meat in a kettle, like flesh in a cauldron (Mic. 3:1–3).

The Lord will not hear them "because they have made their deeds evil." The Lord's judgment is clear on the injustice in the cities.

The voice of the Lord cries to the city—and it is sound wisdom to fear thy name: Hear, O tribe and assembly of the city!

Can I forget the treasures of wickedness in the house of the wicked, and the scant measure that is accursed?

Shall I acquit the man with wicked scales and with a bag of deceitful weights?

Your rich men are full of violence; your inhabitants speak lies and their tongue is deceitful in their mouth.

Therefore I have begun to smite you, making you desolate because of your sins.

You shall eat, but not be satisfied, and there shall be hunger in your inward parts; you shall put away, but not save, and what you save I shall give to the sword.

You shall sow, but not reap; you shall tread olives, but not anoint yourselves with oil; you shall tread grapes, but not drink wine (Mic. 6:9–15).

This is so true today of the exploiters in the big metropolises. We have developed economically, but are barbaric in our relationships with each other. Hence there is deep unrest in our times. The oppressed are unhappy because of their misery. The oppressing one-third of humanity are dehumanized in their ill-gotten affluence.

The Lord shows his utter dissatisfaction with the worship and offerings of the unjust:

With what shall I come before the Lord, and bow myself before God on high? Shall I come before him with burnt offerings, with calves a year old?

Will the Lord be pleased with thousands of rams, with ten thousands of rivers of oil? Shall I give my first-born for my transgression, the fruit of my body for the sin of my soul? (Mic. 6:6–7).

He then shows what is the way of true righteousness as well as of worship:

He has showed you, O man, what is good; and what does the Lord require of you but to do justice, and to love kindness and to walk humbly with your God? (Mic. 6:8).

Chapter III

Jesus, the Eucharist, and Human Liberation

In order to understand the Eucharist we have to see the role of Jesus as the Savior in the society of his time and in subsequent history. Like Moses and Aaron he found his people in subjection to the foreign and local rulers of the time. He gave himself to the task of liberating his people. He protested against all wrong religious conventions and the efforts to absolutize privileges of some over others. He worked to break down barriers between social classes and between Israel and the gentile nations. In the process of such teaching and active commitment he had to face public accusations and the possibility of being imprisoned, tried, and put to death. He knew that his enemies were planning to kill him. Many had warned him about it, including his closest disciples.

It was at this stage of his life that Jesus established the Eucharist. He foresaw that he would soon leave his people and his community of followers. He wanted to leave to them a sign, a symbol, a memorial of his life work and a way of being present to them through their own identification with the poor and the suffering. For this he used the symbol and the ceremony for the Jewish Pasch. *He gave the Pasch a new meaning and a wider relevance.* The meaning of the Eucharist was fundamentally in his self-oblation for the cause of integral human liberation. As a meal it was also a symbol of the unity of the participants in the same cause (even though one of them was to betray him). He

16

offered bread and wine in union with his own sacrifice that was soon to be consummated in his death. In the Eucharist we see several aspects. There is first the meal, the celebration of the Jewish Pasch, the festivity which recalls the liberation by God. Second, the presence of Jesus, for, he said, "This is my body." Theologians may elaborate the exact nature of his presence. However, the most important aspect is his presence in inviting us to our own response to his sacrifice and the commitment to the society of our time. Third, and related to these, the Eucharist is the memorial of his passion and death. He does not die any more, but we recall it, we reenact it in ourselves. Fourth, the Eucharist is a renewal of the covenant. "This is my blood of the covenant shed for many" (Mark 14:23). The New Testament is the promise of God to redeem humankind in the blood of Christ. His death is a sign of the new covenant and the principle for its realization. The Eucharist, therefore, has eschatological significance in relating to the ultimate liberation in the kingdom: just as manna related to the liberation of Jews in Jerusalem. The Eucharist is also our response to Christ's invitation to "do this in commemoration of me, for every time you eat this bread and drink this cup you proclaim the death of the Lord until he comes" (1 Cor. 11:26).

To Jesus' mind, the Eucharist was essentially action-oriented. It was a prayer and an offering in the midst of his public life at the height of his involvement in the political and social issues of the time. It signified his irrevocable contestation of the religious leaders of his people and the narrowness of their message.

For him, it was united to a fundamental option to die rather than to live in compromise. It was a calculated risk. He placed his confidence in the survival of his message and spirit even if his body were to be killed. It was a prelude to his agony, the preparation for his betrayal by one who drank of the cup with him.

The Eucharist was also to be the bond of the new community he was establishing in his new spirit.

THE CLEANSING OF THE TEMPLE

Jesus too, like the prophets, showed his utter disapproval and disgust with those who falsified worship. He saw how the temple of Jerusalem had been made a center of trade, of buying and selling; a den of thieves and not a house of true prayer. On this occasion we see the holy anger of Jesus. John testifies that "he made a whip of cords, and he drove them all, with the sheep and oxen, out of the temple; and he poured out the coins of the money-changers and overturned their tables" (John 2:15–17).

This action of Jesus was against the economic exploitation of the Jewish society and the Roman occupation; but it was also a clear condemnation of the corruption to which the priesthood of the day had been reduced. The priests did recite long prayers. They celebrated the temple feasts. But they participated in a system in which the temple itself had become a kingpin of business and exploitation. Jesus could not stand this mockery of worship. The priests had collaborated in this distortion of religion and prayer. The temple was guarded by the Roman soldiers as a central institution of the whole socio-political edifice of their colonial exploitation.

Thus when Jesus attacked the vendors in the temple and forcibly chased them away with all their goods, he was challenging the whole military, business, and religious power complex of the day. After this operation Jesus continued to teach daily in the temple. He would have evidently proposed an alternative teaching and example to the people. Luke tells us that "the chief priests and the scribes and the principal men of the people sought to destroy him; but they did not find anything they could do, for all the people hung upon his words" (Luke 19:47–48). According to Mark, too, this was one of the reasons the chief priests and scribes wanted to destroy him, "for they feared him, because all the multitude was astonished at his teaching" (Mark 11:18).

From this incident we see how concerned Jesus was that the place of worship should not be prostituted for exploitation in business—to be "a den of thieves." He naturally fell foul of the clergy who acquiesced in this—or perhaps even benefited from it. *The purification of prayer was also a political act.* It upset the scribes and principal men of the area. For the whole system held together. His action was not only opposed to this distortion of worship and extortion of money. Positively he taught what true worship is. This was accepted by the people. His temple teaching was a liberation to the people—from the false worship and from fear of the merchants, scribes, leaders, soldiers, and high priests. The people appreciated this. They understood his message. They "hung on his lips." They responded warmly to such genuine worship, which was also liberating them as persons and as a people.

From this incident we can also see how closely related his prophetic action concerning worship was to his own death. He was murdered by the combination of all the forces that profited by the trade in the temple. He risked the displeasure and hatred of the high priests—the accredited religious leadership of his people. They were unfortunately in close alliance with the traders and colonizers. They had evidently presented a form of religion that did not contest their evils. When these nefarious elements saw that Jesus was literally and even physically upsetting their business, they decided to destroy him. This is not something new in Jewish history or in the world. The prophets were destroyed one after the other. Today, too, we see this phenomenon. Someone contesting exploiting merchants is got rid of. If one brings such matters up in a church one is regarded as going outside the scope of religion. She or he is accused of being "political," "divisive," "sowing hatred." Few are the high priests even today who would side with such a person and not with the exploiting persons.

The cleansing of the temple is an important lesson for our times too. It shows the close relationship among worship, economics, and politics. Even today we have to reflect how much the financial aspects connected with prayer and worship may be having an influence on the life of the churches. How far are novenas, devotions, and pilgrimages genuinely spiritual, and how far are they conditioned by the income generated by them? This is the constant temptation for the clergy of all times, and we should do well to keep Jesus' action in mind. Our attachment to gain may distort our worship and dilute the radicality of the Gospel.

THE PRAYER OF JESUS

Jesus wanted the prayer of his followers to be honest, sincere, serious, and related to real life rather than merely to external formulae, ritual, or convention. For prayer to be authentic, it had to relate to action. He was against hypocrisy in prayer. He did not believe in the multiplication of prayers, in the increase of their volume or frequency. He warned against the tendency of words without seriousness of purpose. Nor was his prayer one that required sacred places, times, vestments, words, ceremonies, or persons. For him the sacredness of prayer was its sincerity and its integrity.

In the Eucharist we see Jesus in prayer. It was a prayer that was said at a meal, in the company of apostles. The ceremony was that of a Jewish festivity that every family could celebrate. There was no priestly garment, no sacred vessel. What he brought to it as exceptional was his commitment to the cause of integral human liberation for which he was offering his life. The first Eucharist was, therefore, an event apart from synagogue or temple, in which the offering of one's life out of love for one's fellow human beings was the constituent element. His discourse before it emphasizes such love in commitment, service, and fellowship. The priest was also the victim. If there was a pre-eminence in his priesthood, it was in service, and in first offering himself as a victim.

Jesus offered the Eucharist only once. It was not something to be easily repeated, to be multiplied without much meaning and serious thought. For him it was so full of meaning that it was not necessary for him to offer it twice. We might even say that since he fulfilled what it symbolized by giving his life he could *not* offer it twice. It was his supreme prayer, symbol, and prelude to his total self-giving for the liberation of his people and eventually of all humankind.

We have to be careful that we do not try to make up for an absence of commitment and seriousness by all manner of other means, such as increasing the frequency of celebration, by ritualization, through growth of a priestly caste that alone is capable of presiding, through the construction of big buildings where the Eucharist is to be offered with use of colorful and rich vestments, the accompaniment of beautiful music, the display of decorations, or the gathering of vast crowds. All these can be useful if there is a meaning. If, on the other hand, the eucharistic celebration does not lead to commitment, to personal and societal liberation in a serious manner, then all these externals are a mere distraction, a dissipation of energy, and a lessening of the real meaning of Eucharist. In fact, it may even be suspect whether these are not an indication of the absence of a seriousness of commitment.

We may ask ourselves how it is possible that societies calling themselves Christian can offer the Eucharist weekly, for years, without improving the relationships among persons in it. What would be the meaning of fifty-two Masses offered during a year in a city if as a result of it there were no effort at bridging the immense gulf that separates the rich in their mansions and the poor in the shanties? Is not the Eucharist a part of the sacrament of unity? St. Paul himself complained bitterly that those who participated in the Eucharist were not tending toward unity. "If you receive the body and blood of Christ unworthily, do you not receive judgment unto yourself?"

It was such an understanding of the Eucharist that made Paul critical of the abuses that were creeping in among the Corinthians even in those early days. He wanted the Eucharist to be a real sharing in mind and goods and therefore he says that the eucharistic community is to form one body: "When we break the bread, is it not a means of sharing the body of Christ? Because there is one loaf, we, many as we are, are one body; for it is one loaf of which we all participate" (1 Cor. 10:16–17). He continues: "Anyone who eats the bread or drinks the cup of the Lord unworthily will be guilty of desecrating the body and blood of the Lord" (1 Cor. 11:27).

The Eucharist is spiritual food insofar as it leads to greater love, self-unity, and communion among persons and groups. Today this requires love among persons and an effective action for justice. The Eucharist must also lead us to a response to the suffering of the masses, often caused by people who take a prominent part in the Eucharist. Unless there is this twofold dimension of personal love and societal action, the Eucharist can be a sacrilege.

Chapter IV

The Cult of the Eucharist
over the Centuries

THE EARLY CHRISTIANS AND THE FATHERS

The Eucharist had an important place in the life of the early Christians, who had personal knowledge of Jesus. The Acts of the Apostles describes these eucharistic gatherings in which there was the communal meal as well as "the breaking of bread," referring to the Eucharist. The early Christians met often for this common feast. They gathered in the private houses of fellow Christians. There was a great informality in the event. They listened to the teaching of the apostles, they prayed together, they conversed about their own problems, they shared a meal and commemorated the Lord.

The Eucharist also had to have a close relation to their own personal and social lives. The Acts of the Apostles describes how the early Christians shared all their possessions. This was connected with their concern for others and for the teaching of Jesus.

They met constantly to hear the apostles teach, and to share the common life, to break bread, and to pray. A sense of awe was everywhere, and many marvels and signs were brought about through the apostles. All whose faith had drawn them together held everything in common: they would sell their property and possessions and make a general distribution as the need of each required. With one mind they kept up their daily attendance at the temple, and, breaking bread in private houses, shared their meals with unaffected joy, as they praised God and enjoyed the favor of the whole people. And day by day the Lord added to their number those whom he was saving (Acts 2:42–47).

The very nature of the Christian life was different then. To be a Christian meant *belonging to a movement*. It was a movement which was said "to turn the world upside down" (Acts 17:6). Paul upset the silversmith Demetrius in Ephesus. The silversmiths had a big sale of silver shrines of Diana. Demetrius roused up his fellow businessmen by inciting them against Paul who, he said, "is telling the people that gods made by human hands are not gods at all. There is danger for us here; it is not only that our line of business will be discredited, but also that the sanctuary of the great goddess Diana will cease to command respect" (Acts 19:26–27). Here we see the connection between business and a false religiosity. Paul's preaching had definitely contested this exploitation of the people by wealthy businessmen behind a religious façade.

The life of the early Christians was thus socialistic in sharing their goods. The Eucharist was intimately related to this fellowship. In fact, in the first letter to the Corinthians Paul rebukes those who partake in the Eucharist but do not share their meals:

. . . The result is that when you meet as a congregation, it is impossible for you to eat the Lord's Supper, because each of you is in such a hurry to eat his own, and while one goes hungry another has too much to drink. Have you no homes of your own to eat and drink in? Or are you so contemptuous of the church of God that you shame its poorer members? What am I to say? Can I commend you? On this point certainly not! (1 Cor. 11:20–22).

In this he says, "Your meetings tend to do more harm than good" (1 Cor. 11:17). Then, too, it was not an easy thing for persons to accept others as equals. But the Christians insisted on it. The Eucharist had no meaning if it was not egalitarian and building real community. Paul has a severe judgment on those who thus desecrated the Lord's Supper. The early Christians thus understood the deep meaning of the symbol instituted by Jesus. Its social impact was the main criterion of its value and credibility. That is why the early Christians were so acceptable to many, especially the poor, and so detested by some of the powerful, particularly the exploiters. Christianity was then a dynamic movement of human liberation from selfishness and exploitation. All were to be equal in the believing community and this was symbolized by the eucharistic meal. This was not an easy ideal. There were grave deficiencies, as in the case of Ananias and Saphira, the couple who tried to dupe the community by pretending to share everything. This was a spirituality developed in the raw of life, in a situation of contestation and persecution. Lay women and men lived this spirituality. It was only later that the Eucharist and Christian spirituality began to be monopolized by the clergy and monks and confined to monasteries. This was really a decadence of Christian life and witness from its pristine vitality.

From the times of the apostles there are evidences indicating the social consciousness of the early Christians. This was related to the Eucharist. They were continuing the tradition of the prophets of the Old Testament, and of Jesus, Paul, John, and James in the New Testament. Thus:

Share everything with your brother. Do not say, "It is private property." If you share what is everlasting, you should be that much more willing to share things which do not last. . . .
On the Lord's day, gather in community to break bread and offer thanks. But confess your sins first, so that your sacrifice may be a pure one. No one who has a quarrel with his brother may join your gathering, not until they are reconciled. Your sacrifice must not be made unholy (The Didache, first century A.D.).

The rich take what belongs to everyone, and claim they have the right to own it, to monopolize it. . . .
What keeps you from giving now? Isn't the poor man there?

Aren't your own warehouses full? Isn't the reward promised? The command is clear: The hungry man is dying now, the naked man is freezing now, the man in debt is beaten now—and you want to wait until tomorrow? "I am not doing any harm," you say! "I just want to keep what I own, that is all." . . . You are like someone who sits down in a theatre and keeps everyone else away, saying that what is there for everyone's use is his own. . . . If everyone took only what he needed and gave the rest to those in need, there would be no such thing as rich or poor. After all, didn't you come into life naked; and won't you return naked to the earth? . . .

The bread in your cupboard belongs to the hungry man; the coat hanging unused in your closet belongs to the man who needs it; the shoes rotting in your closet belong to the man who has no shoes; the money which you put in the bank belongs to the poor. You do wrong to everyone you could help, but fail to help (St. Basil, A.D. 330–379).

The price of the kingdom is the food you give to those who need it (St. Leo the Great, A.D. 390–461).

Christians love one another. They never fail to help widows; they save orphans from those who would hurt them. If a man has something, he gives freely to the man who has nothing. If they see a stranger, Christians take him home and are happy, as though he were a real brother. They don't consider themselves brothers in the usual sense, but brothers instead through the Spirit, in God. And if they hear that one of them is in jail, or persecuted for professing the name of their redeemer, they all give him what he needs. If it is possible, they bail him out. If one of them is poor and there isn't enough food to go around, they fast several days to give him the food he needs. . . . *This is really a new kind of person. There is something divine in them* (Aristides, a non-Christian, defending the Christians before Hadrian).

Do you wish to honor the Body of Christ? Do not despise him when he is naked. Do not honor him here in the church building with silks, only to neglect him outside, when he is suffering from cold and from nakedness. For he who said, "This is my Body" is the same who said, "You saw me, a hungry man, and you did not give me to eat." Of what use is it to load the table of Christ? Feed the hungry and then come and decorate the table. You are making a golden chalice and you do not give a cup of cold water? The

Temple of your afflicted brother's body is more precious than this Temple (the church). The Body of Christ becomes for you an altar. It is more holy than the altar of stone on which you celebrate the holy sacrifice. You are able to contemplate this altar everywhere, in the street and in the open squares (St. John Chrysostom). Much later, in the early Middle Ages, we find St. Bernard emphasizing the same perspectives. Instead of merely admiring the beauty and aesthetics of Gothic churches, he said: "Thus wealth is drawn up by ropes of wealth, thus money bringeth money.... O vanity of vanities, yet no more vain than insane! The church is resplendent in her walls, beggarly in her poor. She clothes her stones in gold and leaves her sons naked."

THE PRIVATIZATION OF THE EUCHARIST

During the early centuries of Christianity, the Eucharist was a corporate public worship of the whole community of believers. There would be one celebration in one area. The faithful, including the priests, would gather round the bishop or elder chosen for the purpose. The liturgy was a bond of union among the believers. It was also an occasion for them to initiate new members and relate to the issues of the day. There was an intimate bond between the people and the celebrant. The altar was not distant, as in the big basilicas. There was an ongoing dialogue between the participants. All understood the texts read and the prayers recited. Greek was used because it was the language known at the time. The prayer was not individualistic, but communitarian. The very persecution of the church brought the Christians together. It was often a risky thing to participate in the Eucharist. The sense of being members of one body in Jesus Christ was very strong among believers. Thus the social and collective nature of the Eucharist was lived then. All shared in the eucharistic bread as a sign of the communion among themselves in Jesus. The early Fathers of the church instructed the faithful chiefly around the Eucharist, for example, the sermons of St. Augustine.

Whereas the early liturgy was warm and communi-

tarian, we see that by the end of the first millennium
—the year 1100—a drastic change had taken place in the
liturgy. There is a big gap in the recorded history of the
church in the five centuries from about A.D. 600 to about
A.D. 1100. This was the time of the settling down of the
invaders from the north and the east (the so-called Barbarians) in the areas of the Roman Empire. It was a period
of a certain eclipse of learning and culture in Europe. But
it was also a long creative period when the beginnings of
the modern European nations were being slowly
fashioned. The church had an important role in that phase
of European history.

THE CLERICALIZATION OF THE EUCHARIST

By the year 1100 the Eucharist had a completely different form and meaning. By this time it had become
clericalized. The priest was the all-important functionary
of the Eucharist. He recited the prayers in an alien
tongue—Latin. Most people did not understand it. He said
the prayers silently from an altar that was separated from
the people. He did not face them. He was regarded as the
interpreter of the people to God Almighty. He was the holy
person interceding on behalf of a sinful, unworthy people.
He was alone at the altar, like Moses on the mountain,
conversing with God. The people did not participate in the
action of the Eucharist. They were encouraged to meditate
on the passion of Christ or the lives of the saints. But the
Eucharist was not a creative event in which they all
shared within their own life situations and in concrete
circumstances.

The liturgy and traditions concerning the Eucharist
have been so developed within the Roman Catholic church
that the church has been made totally dependent on the
priests as the ministers of cult. It is a priest alone who can
make Christ present in the form of bread and wine. Traditional discipline was that he alone could touch the
Eucharist and distribute it. He can receive these powers
only from the bishops, who may even deny him the right to

exercise them. Therefore, lay people could not be ministers of the Eucharist. Women were thought incapable by their sex to be ministers of the Eucharist. The rite of the ordination of the priests emphasized very much this cultic form of the ministry. In the parishes the daily presence of the priest is required because of those who want to frequent the Eucharist. It was therefore made a rule of life that priests should offer the Eucharist every day, and until recently this could be only in the mornings. The whole lifestyle of the priest also was largely determined by the necessity of this performance of the ritual.

The Eucharist was not regarded as the action of the people, but rather of God through the intermediary of the priest. The priest gave his faculties in the service of God. God became present in the midst of the people at the Eucharist. The accent was on the worship of the Lord present in the host. Adoration replaced sharing, the following of Jesus, his giving of himself. Communion had become very rare by this time. People received only on certain feast days. Some never received Communion. They felt unworthy of so great a God. The fear of God was stronger than the sense of loving partnership. Only the clergy could touch the sacrament. The laity were a sinful mass of people excluded from the sanctuary.

Such a situation was a consequence of the individualistic approach to religion and the Eucharist. Dom Herwegen, a former abbot of Maria Laach Monastery in Germany, explains this as a turning from an objective to a subjective kind of piety. The authentic spirit of the liturgy is objective and communitarian. It is social and connected with the building of the values of the kingdom of God in real life. But here it is an all-absorbing subjectivism. "This tendency goes along with a shift of emphasis from the union of the whole Church with God to an emphasis on the union of the individual soul with Him" (Louis Boyer, *Life and Liturgy* [New York, 1962], p. 17). The eclipse of the doctrine of the whole church as forming the body of Christ is partly responsible for this individualism and subjectivism.

Even more important was the attitude toward Jesus Christ. In the early centuries Jesus was regarded more as a brother, a human being who was divine, one who gave an example to be followed, one who was interested in the whole community and the human family. The emphasis was less on worship and more on fellowship, less on distance and more on discipleship. But by the early Middle Ages the emphasis was on the divinity of Jesus. This was partly a reaction against widespread heresies such as Arianism, which denied the divinity of Christ. Hence the stress on the worship of Jesus in the Eucharist. He is to be adored in the sacrament, more than followed in his sacrifice. The whole mission of Jesus as one who came to serve others rather than to reign was neglected. He was seen as the Lord and King and less as the one who showed us the way to struggle for more meaningful human lives.

This Christology was basic to much of the individualism and subjectivism of this type of piety. The neglect of the humanity of Jesus meant also an eclipse of the church as the mystical body of Christ. When the oneness and unity of the church was downgraded, there was no equality for the laity. They did not have a role in the Eucharist. They were nonentities, often not even recipients. They were passive spectators. The clergy was all-important. The monks were also the teachers and learned people of the day. The laity were preached to and prayed for. There was a tendency to consider sexual relations as an impediment to approaching the Eucharist.

We can thus understand the proliferation of secondary devotions, which were more intelligible to the people. Meditation on the passion of Jesus and the lives of the saints was encouraged. The feasts of saints became all-important. The veneration of the relics of saints was widespread. Novenas, octaves for saints, and big feasts filled the liturgical calendar. Indulgences were made available for those who contributed toward church finances.

Since the Eucharist was regarded as an action of God, the people had little responsibility for it. They could, however, "apply" the merits of a Mass for the souls in purgatory. This could be done by prayer or by paying a stipend for a Mass. Then the church would use its mediation for the benefit of the souls for whom the Mass was offered. There was a certain automatism in this, a type of magic. Dom Godfrey Dickmann, O.S.B., records that "the Mass to a frightening degree became an *automatic device* for obtaining favours, spiritual and temporal" *(Come, Let Us Worship* [London, 1962], p. 18).

It was this type of abuse that led Martin Luther to denounce the Mass as then practiced as "spiritual traffic based on clerical cupidity." Even the Agenda Committee of the Council of Trent stated "among the causes which, to put it mildly, have brought about a general weakening of the power of the Mass, two stand out most prominently: *superstition and avarice"* (ibid., p. 19). This is a strong condemnation from a council which undertook the remedying of the evils that caused the Reformation. Superstition in the simple believers and avarice in those who benefit from their superstition are a permanent danger for all religious institutions. J. A. Jungmann, S.J., observes how all these things deeply compromised the faith. "Again we are bound to lay bare a dissolution at the heart of ecclesiastical and liturgical life. What remains firm is on the fringe. To begin with faith is not disturbed. *But the things men are living by are fragments of faith, peripheral things.* Veneration of the saints and their relics—genuine or faked—is often quite unrestrained. Protections and blessings are sought in ever new ways; the rituals became full of new benedictions" *(Pastoral Liturgy,* 1962, p. 79). The great popularity of the Protestant Reformation is understandable against such a background. It was a strong protest following centuries of abuse. We have to see it as an effort to restore the purity of the faith, even though it too had its excesses.

The theory of the quasi-automatic conferring of grace by the mere action of the priest at the Mass *(ex opere operato)* was partly the cause and partly the effect of this privatization and clericalization of the Eucharist. This theory of the causality of the sacraments gave a very great importance to the clerical state. It was the clergy alone who would thus bestow God's grace. The bounty of God had to be channeled through the good offices of ecclesiastical officials. When we take into account the hold that the Christian religion had on the whole western world during the thousand years of the Middle Ages we can imagine what a spiritual power this meant. They did not have to face the problem of other religions, or of "salvation outside the church." Ecclesiastical power was supreme in the spiritual sphere. The fear of eternal damnation helped to maintain this control over souls.

This theory of causality of the sacraments is different from the earlier one of the sacraments being a sign of the grace they confer. Sacraments in this view indicate the type of grace but do not automatically confer it. The human agent or recipient and his or her dispositions are also important for the conferring of grace. This is a theological discussion which has had great significance over the centuries. Two different views of theology flow from them. Today there is a tendency to return to the importance of the active participation of all concerned. In fact the trend is to go back to the spiritual view that the sacraments can even be counterproductive if they are not backed up by the good life of the faithful, especially in relation to social justice. Hence also the questioning of the value of mere presence at the Eucharist on Sundays without there being an effective impact on personal and societal relationships.

The Catholic reaction to the Protestant challenge was to tighten the rules concerning the liturgy and emphasize the importance of the clergy and of the authority in the church. Luther emphasized the significance of the laity. He spoke of the priesthood of the laity. He stressed the personal nature of religion and worship. He advocated the use of the vernacular in the liturgy. To these the Catholics responded with more orthodoxy in the sense of defending

ecclesiastical authority and the causality of the sacraments in themselves. This tended to give Catholic liturgy a
great rigidity and uniformity. For centuries the Catholic
church could not get away from it. The Latin Mass was
obligatory all over the Catholic world. The translation of
the prayers of the Mass from Latin to the vernaculars was
forbidden by Pope Alexander VII in 1661. This prohibition
was renewed by Pope Pius IX as late as 1857. It was tacitly
dropped under Pope Leo the XIII in 1897. Vatican II reversed the decision (1962) and encouraged the use of the
vernacular.

THE NEGLECT OF SHARING

For Jesus the Eucharist was the supreme symbol of his
self-offering unto death. But over the centuries the Christian tradition has largely diluted or neglected this. The
accent has, rather, been on the real presence of Christ
under the form of bread and wine and in the tabernacle.
This had taken place already in the first centuries of the
church when Christianity became the religion of the established society. Churches were built in villages, royal
places, and monasteries. There was a custom of reserving
of the blessed sacrament. The monks of the ninth and
tenth centuries propagated devotion for the Mass as a
means of saving souls from purgatory. The teaching was
that each Mass was capable of gaining a certain amount of
merit, and Gregorian Masses were more valuable. High
Masses and sung Masses got more souls out of purgatory
than ordinary Masses. To these corresponded the stipend
offered by the faithful. The value of the Eucharist was
made to depend on the number of Masses offered. It was a
quantitative approach to salvation. The quality and inten-
sity of the offering were neglected.

The adoration of the blessed sacrament was made a central element by Catholic spirituality, especially in contrast
to certain Protestant churches, which contested the real
presence. The religious spent long hours before the tabernacle. Parishes organized "forty-hours" adoration. It was

that Jesus was a prisoner of the tabernacle, that he needed consolation, that he was lonely. Great preachers like Father Mateo Crawley-Boevey popularized such points of view. While one may reflect on Jesus in this manner, we know that in Jesus' life the Eucharist had quite a different meaning. It was related to the liberation and salvation of humanity.

The Eucharist was regarded sometimes as a means with which to bless people, once again without reference to its essential meaning. Devotions such as the benediction of the blessed sacrament were major events of parish life. The benedictions of the blessed sacrament were almost totally devoid of a relationship to human society. In fact, there were stereotype hymns often repeated, like the *Tantum Ergo*, which had to be sung in Latin at every benediction almost everywhere in the world. The devotions had become so formal that there was a strong conviction that this could not be changed. The devotion to the Eucharist was made heavenly and ethereal. It was regarded as the food of angels, or of human beings without much reference to their bodies and their earthly concerns.

Eucharistic devotion was extremely ritualized, especially in the Catholic tradition. The Sacred Congregation of Rites in Rome claimed a monopoly on how the Eucharist was to be celebrated. For centuries they determined the minute details of the celebration, for example, the type of bread to be used, the type of wine, the percentage of alcohol in the wine, the water, the dress, the ceremony. Sometimes the wine had to be brought from Europe to the Asian countries to satisfy these requirements. The church authority, like the bishops, spent a good deal of time maintaining these rules. The formation of priests was then closely related to the knowledge of the eucharistic ritual, with slight variations permitted for certain days. This meant a uniformity all over the world; Catholics gloried in such uniformity. Thus the Eucharist was a highly organized form of prayer. Anything not in Latin and not controlled by the traditional rubrics could not be liturgical.

The official prayer of the church had to be uniform all over the world, even if not one percent of the people understood it. "Liturgy ran the risk of becoming a subject for rubrical antiquarianism, an aesthetic show piece" (Jungmann, *Pastoral Liturgy*, p. 91).

It was also made a matter of obligation. All the Catholics of a locality had to go to a particular type of church in order to satisfy a Sunday obligation. This was linked to attendance at Sunday Mass, being made obligatory under pain of sin. The emphasis then was on the extent of the Mass to be heard to fulfill the Sunday obligation. Fidelity to this practice was regarded as a sign of Catholic faithfulness. This could be an external and purely formal understanding of religion which seems to merit the reproach Christ made concerning the formalism of the religion of his day.

The traditional eucharistic devotion was cut off from the life of the people and from their day-to-day problems. The numbers present at the Eucharist and the utterly heterogeneous character of the congregation in the church did not permit any common reflection for action. Thus it had little or no positive impact on Christians regarding their social obligations. It divorced them from real life. But since it was regarded as the main item of Christian piety it had the impact of satisfying people in their need to believe that they were good. They could do anything outside the church, and Sunday Mass gave them the feeling of being forgiven and blessed by the custodians of God's graces.

The Eucharist was also to some extent subject to commercialization due to the payment for the Masses in varying amounts and the collections made during the Mass. In certain countries several collections are taken. It is true that money is needed for the cult and upkeep of the ministers, but this tended to be a way in which money could be collected for the purposes of the religious establishment.

Sometimes eucharistic devotion was in complete silence, as inside cloisters of religious; but at other times there were triumphal demonstrations, as at eucharistic congresses. But traditionally both these were cut off from relationship to the actual problems facing people in society.

The history of Catholic spirituality has for many centuries adopted this pietistic, individualistic approach. It is only now that there is an effort at some sort of breakthrough.

The teaching of the book *The Imitation of Christ* gives us an idea of this individualistic, otherworldly approach of Christians toward the Eucharist.

The emphasis in the theology of the Eucharist was on its effect *ex opere operato*, that is, from the work done by its very nature irrespective of the conditions of the person performing it. It therefore neglected the personal element in the eucharistic celebration, namely, *ex opere operantis*. Thus the Eucharist tended to be a mechanical ceremony under the control of the priests without much impact on the relationships of persons. Rich and poor, exploiter and exploited, colonizer and colonized, good and bad were all present at the same Eucharist and received Communion without challenging or questioning their relative positions. This, of course, is quite contrary to the teachings of Jesus in the Gospel. As such there was a neglect of the elements of victimhood, sacrifice, commitment, and communion.

This type of eucharistic celebration existed for centuries during which the Christians were involved in internecine wars against the Muslims or among themselves or against the poor peoples of America, Asia, and Africa. The theory of salvation then was such that the Eucharist could be offered in the morning and soldiers could then go to battle to kill the natives and aborigines of these countries, especially if they refused to be baptized.

THE EUCHARIST, CAPITALISM, AND COLONIALISM

Over the centuries the spirituality of the Eucharist—of giving and not of grabbing—was obliterated. The Euch-

arist went side by side with the worst and largest-scale
exploitation that the world has ever seen. The tragedy of
the subordination of Christianity to European power politics was also the tragedy of the Eucharist. As the priests
and monks went hand in hand with the colonialists, the
Eucharist was desecrated in the service of empire. The
Eucharist was (one hopes unconsciously) perverted in the
close alliance between imperialism and the church. Gold
grabbed from the native people of South America was used
to adorn Christian monasteries and churches, as in Lima,
Peru. The gold used to decorate the ceiling of the Basilica
of Saint Mary Major in Rome is claimed to have been
brought from the new territories conquered for the Christian rulers and religion. These are symbols of the low level
to which religion had sunk in the Europe of the colonial
period. Hence we must not be so naive as to accept as
"faith" whatever beliefs or practices prevail at any given
time concerning the Eucharist. We must not think that the
so-called simple faith of the people is innocent in itself. It
has been evolved alongside the world's worst exploitation
and did not contest it or, rather, it tended to justify the
status quo.

At the beginning of the twentieth century Pope Pius X
popularized the reception of the Eucharist. Children were
admitted to Communion at the age of reason, that is, seven
years. Frequent Communion was encouraged. But there
was no emphasis on the social dimension of the Eucharist.
This was still largely the individualistic phase of the Mass
and the sacraments. The vast popularization of the reception of Communion may have spread individual devotion,
but it did not make the sacrament a greater sign and cause
of real unity in the Christian community or the world at
large.

In the nineteenth and twentieth centuries the growth
and development of the technologically superior countries
went hand in hand with the large-scale exploitation of the
proletariat in the rich countries and all of the people in the
poor countries. The eucharistic ceremony did not disturb

the peace of conscience of the exploiting capitalists; it tended to legitimize their nefarious activities. The prayers offered by the faithful were conducive to internalizing the relationships that were being built up within the emerging societies.

It is therefore understandable that increasingly the working classes in the European countries began to keep away from the Sunday Eucharist, for they did not see in the ceremony anything they were hoping for in their struggles against the human exploitation by their Christian overlords. For the Eucharist had become a means of helping the affluent people of the world.

It is not surprising that the working classes in Western Europe were "dechristianized" during the course of the past few centuries. Being Christian was judged by attendance at Sunday Mass: this was the concept of a "practicing" Catholic. The Mass was unrelated to the struggles of the exploited working classes. It even helped in their exploitation; it contributed to their mental subjugation. It was a sort of opium of the exploited. Workers and their exploiters attended Mass side by side. Yet there was no unity; no communion. The exploitation continued. The priests generally preached obedience and submission on the part of the workers, and charity and paternalism by the capitalists. Gradually many workers dropped away from the Sunday Mass. Later on, they did not care to have their children baptized. For the Christian group had lost its real meaning as a community of loving sharing.

If the Eucharist is the center of Christian living, its evacuation of meaning was a cause and effect of the irrelevance of Christianity to people's central concerns as person and social being. When the Eucharist ceases to relate to integral human liberation, it ceases to be connected with Christ's life sacrifice; it does not then build human community; it does not, therefore, help constitute the kingdom of God on earth; it does not even honor God objectively. It becomes a ritual without life, like the type of sacrifices condemned by God in the Old Testament.

On the other hand, as Christianity gets revitalized, the Eucharist, its chief act of worship and sacrifice, acquires meaning and relevance. It is thus that we have in the contemporary Christian renewal a revaluation of the Eucharist.

Vatican Council II helped very much toward the updating of the eucharistic liturgy. It made possible alterations in the language of the liturgy, in its choice of more suitable Gospel texts. It simplified the ceremonial and made it less rigid. The council invited a greater participation of the faithful in the Eucharist. It encouraged the adaptation of the liturgy to the customs and culture of the peoples.

At the same time, the council left all control over the liturgy and its changes in the hands of the authorities in Rome and the local bishops. During the past twelve years the official church has gradually embarked on effecting these changes, but usually with a certain reluctance and caution.

However, today the main trends in the evolution of the eucharistic theology and devotion take place outside the official circles concerned with the control of the Eucharist, that is, the Roman curia and the local diocesan authorities. It is groups that are engaged as Christians in the active search for personal and societal liberation that are spearheading new approaches toward the Eucharist. These insist on the celebration being truthful, authentic, forming community, leading to action, and increasing genuine sharing among persons and groups. In participating in the sacrifice of Christ, they find inspiration and strength in their efforts to be more authentic persons committed to the integral liberation of persons.

While the churches have been going through this painful, slow, and piecemeal adjustment in the eucharistic rite, the world of business has come into a new and frightening phase. Today the situation is quite different from that of thirty years ago or even of 1962 when the Vatican Council adopted its Constitution on the Liturgy. Since then the cold war between the capitalist West and the socialist countries of Eastern Europe has virtually come to an end. "Detente" is the order of the day in their relationships. Likewise the western powers are coming to terms with Communist China. The war in Vietnam is over; most of Southeast Asia and Latin America are under military dictatorships. Africa has been politically liberated except in the south. Spain and Portugal have reaffirmed their desire for more freedom with a touch of socialism.

A more significant factor is the increasing power of the transnational corporations with their headquarters in North America, Western Europe, and Japan. A few hundred enormous companies dominate world economic activities. A new mode of exploitation of the masses of Asia, Africa, and Latin America and of workers in Europe, North America, Japan, and Oceania has become a major factor in the world. The inequalities are growing within and among nations. The concentration of economic, political, and cultural power in the hands of the captains of industry, commerce, and finance is unprecedented in human history. The East-West detente may give them a freer hand to exploit the poor. They now penetrate the European socialist countries also. The local elites of the so-called Third World cooperate with them in the exploitation of their own lands and peoples.

New alliances are being formed across national frontiers. The powerful in the rich West, in Eastern European socialist countries, and in the "free world" in Africa, Asia, and Latin America are joining hands to maintain and improve their positions. The exploited everywhere are groaning in their misery. Many workers, youth, and women feel alienated by this entire process. Liberation struggles are going on in the political, economic, and cultural fronts. The socialist countries help these forces of liberation while preserving international peace in Europe.

A much more fundamental rethinking of the total situation within each society and a radical option for just relations among persons and peoples is called for by this trend in world evolution. The churches move far too slowly in

this fast-changing world. Within fifteen years the transnational corporations have built new empires. They are
"integrating" the world, adjusting it to their "image and
likeness." The eucharistic "reforms" so far carried out by
the official churches are thoroughly inadequate even to
comprehend the issues raised by this rapidly evolving
situation. Much less are they suited to contest the evils
perpetrated today. The new types of exploitation are far
more subtle, sophisticated, and universal than the crude
forms of early capitalist or old colonial exploitation. They
require a response not only in the Eucharist but of the
entire churches and of all persons of good will in the world.

After centuries of evolution, and even after the reforms
of the recent decades, the Eucharist is quite far from relating effectively to the people in the spirit of the teaching of
the Old Testament, of Jesus Christ, and of the early
church. This presents an immense challenge to today's
followers of Jesus Christ everywhere.

Chapter V

The Eucharist in Contemporary Society

Contemporary society has many characteristics which present serious problems to the churches concerning the Eucharist. Some are new issues, others are old questions seen with a new insight and urgency. Some such problems are the quest for meaning and inner fulfillment, the search for community, the concern for justice and human rights in a divided society and world, the emancipation of women, the dialogue of world religions and cultures, and the role of the priesthood. We offer some comments on these in this and subsequent chapters.

THE QUEST FOR PERSONAL MEANING

Almost everywhere in the world human beings are going through a phase in which they seek to know more clearly the meaning of their lives and of what they do. This is partly due to a disillusionment with the world as it is. They feel deceived by different leaders who have brought them to the present mess. The very power of the control over their lives by modern technology makes their spirit search elsewhere for fulfillment. Even the practices of the traditional religions do not measure up to this requirement. They sense the relative emptiness of much external ritual or conformity without inner meaning or conversion.

The widespread interest in Yoga and the meditative practices of the other oriental religions is an indication of the nature of this search. That western society is discovering the value of Yoga is indicative of both the spiritual quest of many in those countries and of their sense of the inadequacy of the spiritual practices of traditional Christianity. The attraction for Buddhism, Hinduism, Yoga, and meditation is fairly widespread in Europe and North America. This cannot be lightly dismissed as some passing phase, or a fanciful taste for the exotic. It indicates that one dimension of the search of contemporary persons is for interiority, quiet, and meaning.

The appeal of Yoga can be understood in the context of the lack of fulfillment that many feel with the conditions of modern life. In the more industrialized societies the external pressures on the individual person are very great. The mass media leave little freedom for the senses. The eyes and ears are continually confronted with things to be seen and heard. The senses of taste and touch are also pampered and pandered to with the growth of affluence. The newspapers, the radio, and especially the television enter right into the homes of most people. They invade the free spaces left to persons for quiet.

This hyperactivity of the senses may bring much information to people from their earliest days. But it does not communicate much wisdom. In fact it tends to block deeper reflection. The senses being continually occupied tend to dissipate the activity of the mind. The mind is made more passive rather than active, creative, and profound. The immediate data offered by the senses can keep the mind at a superficial level of thought. People become conditioned by this continual excitement of the senses. There is a sort of pollution of the sensory and psychic environment. Noise interferes with the calm of the ears. Speed of communication may present many new things rather quickly and superficially. There is an invasion of the privacy of personal lives.

On the other hand, the anonymity of the big cities makes for a sense of loneliness. People seldom share the inner core of their being with others. There is a large measure of self-centeredness in their lives. The growth in the divorce rate tends to increase the lack of sharing even within families. Many children grow up without the care of father or mother or of both. These children lack the sense of being wanted and loved. Even the provision of social services and insurance against unemployment, old age, and sickness leaves little external area for the concern and care of others. The interpersonal relations can be less loving, though there is more personal freedom.

The excitement of the senses in every direction tends in the long run to leave a sense of emptiness and unfulfillment. The type of propaganda for sex discredits the human person—both the female and the male. Affluence leads to an overconsumption of food and drink. Many adults have to try to counteract obesity due to overeating. The media make them aware of the malnutrition of millions of others. They see the whole system as not leading to worthwhile solutions. The self-seeking of parents tends to neglect the children; the independence or "revolt" of youth can disquiet the parents. The more affluent peoples easily complain of life, of boredom. Sometimes there is hardly anyone or anything to live for. They see less of a struggle as they are cushioned by the affluence of their societies. For some the acquisitiveness of their values tends to increase the desire for more and more possessions or privileges or power.

Perhaps all these tensions may explain the search for quiet, for meaning, and for acceptance by others. The other oriental religions have developed methods of counteracting this invasion of the senses and for deepening the meaning of life. Yoga is one such school. It is a training of the senses, the body, and the mind that is intended to increase the self-mastery of persons and their communion with the Absolute. Yoga stresses the importance of control over the senses and of the participation of the physical elements in the psychic process of reflection and meditation.

Yoga is a school of the control and direction of the senses. The disciple can learn concentration of the mind beyond the objects of sense. The multiplicity of objects presented to the senses can be bypassed by a deeper concentration on the essentials, ultimately on the Absolute, the Divine.

Yoga aims at giving a certain tranquillity from outer pressures in order to experience an inner power or force of self and of the Other. It is a form of asceticism. It can strengthen one against ones own passions. It can help a person to counteract the dissipation of the senses. It has a multiplicity of disciplines for training the body and the mind: in posture, in respiration, as well as in thought. Yoga is a process of self-purification leading to deeper meditation, or *Dhyana*. It can give a person a sense of identity and self-possession. The relationship to the Absolute and to others also gives a sense of meaning and purpose.

We can therefore understand why there is a fairly widespread interest in yogic training and meditation in the affluent world. Yoga seems to respond to some of their fundamental needs in a much troubled, though physically saturated environment. It may of course be an escape from social responsibility if it is centered only on the self or even on the Absolute to the neglect of others. There is the danger that the popularity of approaches like Transcendental Meditation (T.M.) may neglect the basic need for social changes. They may pacify executives in corporations by conferring a personal peace in spite of their corporate actions that may make others suffer. This can be a serious danger.

On the other hand, a deeper inner reflection can be associated with a radical social commitment. The two can nourish each other. The example of Mahatma Gandhi stands out pre-eminent in this century. Meditation can provide the motivation and the soul force for resistance to social injustice and for building the alternative society on just relationships. The fight against the acquisitiveness of modern society requires an asceticism in persons and the collectivity. Socialists like Lenin and Mao Tse-tung have insisted on the need of restraints to present consumption for self-reliant growth. Hence there can be a direct link between yogic meditation and the struggle for justice. In this sense the internal spiritual life and the commitment to socio-economic liberation are not contradictory. Rather, they are complementary. There can be no genuine interiority and spirituality that wantonly neglects social justice and compromises with injustice. Self-mastery and holiness should lead to a purification from being an accomplice in the exploitation of others. Otherwise Yoga or "spirituality" can be an alienation from the combat of social sin of our times.

It is not our present intention to develop the theme of Yoga and of meditation in other religions. Rather, we wish to indicate the need for Christian spirituality to relate to the issues posed to contemporary persons by modern society. In this the oriental practices of meditation may teach us how to relate the training of the body and mind to being attuned to the divine and the neighbor.

Since the Eucharist is central to the Christian community and to its spirituality, we have to ask ourselves: Has the Eucharist been able to meet this need, to respond to this dimension of human fulfillment? A deeper problem concerns the meditative practices of the Christian tradition of spirituality: Have these been inadequate and restricted to the religious and clergy? The Mass, especially as celebrated on Sundays in parishes, has been generally very much an externalized ceremony. There is little possibility of quiet meditation at it; or at least it is not fashioned to foster the meditative spirit. There is too much of a concern with externals. The congregation's interest is drawn to different things by the readings, the sermon, the gestures, and also the collections. All these may have a value if they relate to real human concerns. But from the point of view of the need for quiet reflection they can be a distraction. In this sense the Mass does not meet this need. It is hardly a school of spirituality as Yoga and the meditative practices are. It may of course be argued that the practice of the adoration of the Eucharist could provide this need for reflection. This is true. But here too there has been very little development of a method and practice of meditation for lay persons.

The finer inspiration of Christianity concerning the

human body as the temple of the Holy Spirit is not ac-
tuated in the Eucharist as presently celebrated in the
parishes. Christian revelation has an understanding of the
human body that includes several aspects. It is spoken of
as weak and a source of temptation. The body is also the
agent of much good. The care for the corporal needs of
others is a criterion of eternal salvation. The body is to rise
again at the resurrection of the dead to everlasting happiness. For this the body needs disciplining and training. In
the Eucharist all these are given a more specific and
deeper meaning when Jesus says "This is my body" which
is offered for all. His offering of his body is sacrificial,
redemptive, exemplative. It is the will of the Father that in
his contestation of the public evils of the day his body
should be tortured and crucified.

The Christian tradition had in the Middle Ages an accent
on meditation on the body of Christ. There were practices
of corporal asceticism. Monastic meditation was related to
the rhythm of the day and hence of the human body too.
The Gregorian chant, especially of the psalms, provided a
background for a meditative reflection on the word of God.
It also gave time for the sense of the words to penetrate the
inner being of the person. It had a deep meditative mood
and potential.

But the present way of celebrating the Eucharist, especially in big churches, does not really harness its potential
for meditation, for the education and formation of the body
and for giving meaning to life integrally. It is not interior
in the better sense of the word: of being deep, personal,
reflective, and formative. Nor is it external in the good
sense of being active, committed, and transformative of
persons and society. It is externalized and rather ritualis-
tic, but does not have much social commitment. Some con-
fuse spiritual with being passive, and communitarian with
being merely externalized. Hence they cannot easily see
the spiritual dimension of socio-political commitment to
justice. Nor can they appreciate the social demands of
personal holiness. On the other hand, Jesus bears witness

to both and to their interrelation in the Eucharist. His offering of his body is real and definitive. It is the ultimate sacrifice offered in deep prayer and personal reflection. He is conscious of the weight of his cross: "My soul is very sorrowful even unto death; remain here and watch with me. . . . My Father, if it be possible, let this cup pass from me . . ." (Matt. 26:38–39). He does not contest the Jewish high priests and the Roman authorities without serious thinking about it. He is intensively active in his exterior life too. This is linked to his profound personal thought, prayer, and convictions. In prayer he decides to go ahead: "Behold the hour is at hand and the Son of man is betrayed into the hands of sinners. Rise, let us be going; see my betrayer is at hand" (Matt. 26:45–46).

The liturgy of the Word can be a powerful help toward both interior reflection and social commitment. For this there must be a fundamental change in the approach toward the Eucharist. There should be a closer relationship to the public life of Jesus, the Last Supper, and his crucifixion—all of which are intimately linked. It is a pity that those who legislate for the renewal of the liturgy do not pay serious attention to this total relationship. On the other hand, much of the concern of the central church authorities is with a rigid conformity to the rubrics and a quantitative fulfillment of the Sunday obligation. Even the reports required by the Roman Sacred Congregations from local bishops ask for data concerning the number of those who attend Mass or receive Communion. There is much less emphasis, if any at all, on the qualitative and deeper personal and social dimensions of the Eucharist.

THE SEARCH FOR COMMUNITY

Corresponding to the quest for a personal identity as against the alienation of human persons from themselves is the search for being in harmony with others. The desire for community is a strong urge in our day too. Human solidarity is seen as an urgent need. The media bring us news of the lack of brotherliness and sisterliness in the relationships among persons and nations. The world spends about U.S. $300 billion on armaments. When this is taken in the background of the 4 billion dollars a year which the United States offers as "aid" to the world (most of it is military aid and investment) we can try to grasp something of the enormous waste involved in the production of these brutal weapons.

This is only one aspect of the lack of community today. Similar waste can be seen at national levels. The inequalities in the world and within countries make the search for community even more challenging. Within a small group such as a parish, an action group, or a religious community also there is a desire for understanding among persons. To be accepted by others, to be cared for, to be able to love and care for others are basic human needs. They are intensified as needs because of today's widespread isolation and individualism.

Modern "civilization," while being technologically extraordinarily advanced, is utterly inhuman in its concern for others and for nature. We are highly civilized barbarians. We have conquered nature in many aspects. We can communicate to and from other celestial bodies. We can move mountains, cause rain, and overcome many diseases. Humanity was never so skilled as now. We are civilized in that sense. We are also refined in some of our manners of behavior. We know how to talk suavely; we can be polished and diplomatic in our relationships. We have developed the sciences as well as the arts.

Yet we are also barbarians. We can destroy nature, and we do so. We pollute the earth. We kill lakes and seas. We erode mountainsides and plains. We destroy trees, exterminate animals. We produce super-powerful lethal weapons. We trade them. We improve them systematically; we use them for genocide.

We are selfish, greedy, and gluttonous. We have enough food for all men, women, and children on the earth; yet a few of us grab this food for ourselves, our animals, and our garbage cans. We feast while others starve to death. We see this on our television screens and we pass pious resolutions about an ambiguous "aid" to those from whom we steal the food. We go to church on Sunday; we say, "Give us this day our daily bread," but our social and economic options deprive the hungry of food, the multitudes of remunerative work.

We are barbarians, for we steal from the hungry, we rob the famine-stricken. If two out of ten children ate the food of the eight others and gave knives to the half-starved eight to fight each other, we would condemn the children as barbarians. This is the position of the human race today. We the rich countries and the rich of the poor countries are "civilized" but we are barbarians.

Thus, while everywhere in the world society is deeply divided, especially between the rich and the poor, the powerful and the weak, the exploiting and the exploited, the Eucharist as a sacrament of unity should build togetherness or at least tend toward it. It is the sacrament for the nourishment of the spiritual life of those baptized and, hence, must tend to create the values of the kingdom of Christ in which there will be no discrimination as between rich and poor, Jew and gentile, and man and woman. It is also a sacrament of repentance and conversion. In the presence of disunity and discrimination, it should lead us to a deep conversion of hearts and to action for the reformation of society. In this way, the Eucharist is a remedy against selfishness both individual and social and a help in the struggle for building the new human society on earth. Thus the healing power of the blood of Christ is to take effect in society.

Unfortunately, the Eucharist itself has very often been the means of perpetuating injustice and divisions. Different places have been built for worship by different communities, such as different Christian groups, churches, and racial groups. There are different Masses in the same city meant for persons of different social classes. The Masses offered on occasions like weddings and funerals, with the graded charges, are also another means of catering to social divisions. Instead of turning toward repentance, reform, and conversion of heart, these encourage disunity, discrimination, and sometimes exploitation. In certain countries like South Africa there are parishes and services which are meant only for whites and others only for blacks. These are maintained by some without an effort to combat the inequalities and discrimination in the system of apartheid. But what is true of South Africa is often true of the rest of the world even though the situation may not be so blatantly revolting. Further, the Eucharist has the disadvantage of several centuries of linkage with colonial exploitation and its brutality.

Such divisions and injustices are an obstacle to the truthfulness of the celebration of the Eucharist. Often, as a eucharistic community, people are not even aware of the division in their society. This is because eucharistic communities seldom reflect together on the type of society in which they live. There is not much social analysis taking place among participants in the Sunday Eucharist in the parishes. They come there almost as a matter of obligation or by routine. On the other hand, before Jesus celebrated the Eucharist he prepared the apostles, for three years, to understand their mission so that when the Eucharist was offered they were aware of its grave significance. They were even frightened of it. At the end of the eucharistic meal Jesus told the apostles, "Let us now go to the Garden of Olives," and he went afterward to Calvary. Whereas we at our eucharistic gatherings try to finish as early as possible in order to be able to go to our Sunday relaxation and the activities of the rest of the week.

THE LIBERATION OF WOMEN

The Eucharist has been involved in several unfortunate circumstances. It has been associated with Roman imperialism in its latter days, with feudalism, with the rise of capitalism and the spread of colonialism. There is another circumstance to which perhaps not adequate attention is given. The Eucharist, like the rest of religion, has been largely conditioned by male domination of society both among the Jews and in countries that controlled Christianity. Much of what society accepts as normal and even just in the attitudes toward women can thus pass into the practice and teaching concerning the Eucharist with almost a divine sanction by Jesus himself. We see an exclusion of women from responsible action concerning the Eucharist in most Christian churches. How far is this justifiable? Should such a situation be continued until the end of time, all over the globe?

Contemporary emancipation of women has fortunately brought these questions to the fore. The churches, especially the Catholic church, have consequently to face serious issues concerning the Eucharist also. It is noteworthy that the movement for the emancipation of women has emerged and developed without much direct support from the churches. The churches have tended to be the last refuge of male dominance. They have given male chauvinism not only a practical expression, but also a theological and even a quasi-divine legitimation. The Catholic church, once again, can claim to be the most rigid and uncompromising in this respect too.

Women have traditionally been the most faithful supporters of the church and of the eucharistic devotions. Even when the working class was largely dechristianized in Europe and refrained from attending the Sunday Eucharist, the women were much more numerous than the men at the eucharistic services. Without the women many churches would hardly have a congregation. The children are also generally brought by them. Young women often persuade their husbands to return to the sacraments. Women contribute generously to the mainstay of the clergy and of church activities. Women religious are most assiduous in the care of the altar. They give long hours to prayer and work in connection with the eucharistic services.

While women have thus given so much to the cult of the Eucharist, most churches have excluded them from the

priesthood or from any serious responsibility concerning
the eucharistic celebration. They are or were considered
unsuitable due to their sex. Till recently they could not
even read the Scriptures at the services. Girls could not
serve at the altar. Any little boy was preferable to any
female. A certain sense of inferiority or unworthiness concerning the Eucharist was thus ingrained in the women
from their earliest days.

Today, however, the situation is changing. Women are
asserting their rights as human beings. They have advanced in all spheres of life. They are in almost all the
professions in most countries. There are women prime
ministers and cosmonauts. They drive tractors and manage industry. The question is therefore raised as to their
position in the church. Why can they not be priests? Why
can they not preside at the eucharistic sacrifice? Why
should these be male preserves? What in their sex disqual-
ifies them from these functions in the church? They feel
insulted in their very being when they are thus excluded
merely because of their way of being human—namely, as a
female.

Many women still accept the traditional position of the
priestly role being confined to males. They have been conditioned to think and act in that way. Some may even feel
more at ease with a male performing some of these functions than another female. Even if the majority of women
are not conscious of these issues, the more alert and
dynamic among the women dedicated to the cause of
Christ feel that there is here a definite discrimination of a
sexist nature. They are thus hurt in their deepest being.
They are torn between a respect for the church and their
inability to accept such a treatment from a community
which should foster human equality and solidarity. Due to
a sense of loyalty and religiosity they love and accept the
church. On the other hand, their convictions concerning
feminism and their need to combat male chauvinism in its
different ramifications make them somewhat lose their
confidence in the church. Their self-respect makes it dif-

ficult for them to accept the church attitudes with compla-
cency. Yet many do not leave the church or the Eucharist.
But as they grow in awareness of the problem they are ill
at ease within themselves and in the eucharistic gatherings.

The question arises: Is the discipline of the church un-
changeable? Is it merely a matter of a certain social conditioning of the church? Or is it from Christ? If so, was Christ
a misogynist? Does God also favor males? Is sexism in the
church an incurable evil? If so what is the nature of the
church? Should its sexism be combated from within or
should feminists leave the church?

One of the difficulties in this regard is the argument put
forward by some churchmen that they are only following
the example of Jesus. The saying of Paul concerning
women being silent is added for good measure. The history
of the churches is adduced as further corroboration of the
thesis that the priesthood should be confined to males.
While the facts of the case seem to be true, there are many
loopholes in this line of argument.

First of all, it is not clear that Jesus established the
priesthood. The priesthood as it is presently known began
later on in the life of the church. If it is argued that he gave
the power over the Eucharist to his apostles, and that they
are the predecessors of the bishops, then should not the
bishops be the ones to preside over the Eucharist? Why can
bishops confer this power to other males who are priests
and not to any women? Is the male traitor better than the
faithful women who stood by Jesus at the foot of the cross?
Is it not to them that Jesus first revealed himself after his
resurrection? One could further argue that since the apostles were Jews, all bishops should still be Jews, and circumcised. Could the argumentation be continued further to
say that the chief of the bishops should be married, as
Peter was? We ask these questions in order to ask: Where
do we draw the line in following the example of Jesus?
Could it not be possible that the line was drawn on a sex
basis due to the tradition of male domination, rather than

due to any divine inspiration? Even if Jesus chose males as apostles (not priests) how much was this due to the social conditions of the times?

Recently the Vatican Congregation for the Doctrine of the Faith declared that priests should be males in order to be like Jesus. It presupposes that Jesus was an ordained priest of the Christian (or Catholic) church. Jesus was not an ordained minister of the Christian religion. He was a rabbi, a lay teacher among the Jews. Nor did he begin the Christian ordained priesthood. Insofar as he is called the unique high priest of the New Testament, there are to be no other priests like him. He teaches that we can go directly to the Father without any intercessors. Therefore it does not seem to be a valid conclusion from the maleness of Jesus of Nazareth to argue that women cannot be priests in the Catholic church. If this were a valid argument, once again can we not ask whether all priests should not be Jews, circumcised, poor, vagrant . . . like Jesus? And that only males should be at the Eucharist, as at the Last Supper?

Not only is this case rather poor, it is adding insult to injury to women. It is bad enough that women are thus treated in the church; but when the sex characteristics of Jesus are adduced in favor of a male priesthood one can see to what extent male domination can go to suit its own purposes. But this type of argument raises further christological questions. In what sense is Jesus the Christ? Is God a male? Is the Christ, in whom all things are to be resumed on earth and in heaven, a male? Are females a lower species in relation to the divinity?

On the other hand, it could be maintained that very much of the practice and teaching of the Christian churches concerning the priesthood and the male presidency over the Eucharist are the consequence of a male-dominated social system. Jesus himself had to face a similar or even worse situation than we or those of past centuries have had to. There was little respect for women in Jewish society. They were to live as far as possible withdrawn from public life. Men were to converse little with them in public. Men of religion were to be particularly reserved in their dealings with women. In the temple, too, there was discrimination against women; they had access only to the women's forecourt. They were treated in the same way as slaves regarding the obligation of prayer. Men could divorce women easily by simply issuing a writ of divorce.

Jesus was extraordinary in going against these taboos and inhibitions. We do not argue that he foresaw or forestalled all that the Women's Liberation movement of today would do or want. But he was far ahead of his time. He set an example of contesting such male domination. Jesus got away from the custom of having no contact with women. He was friendly to them. He moved freely with them. There were men and women in the company of his followers. Even persons of ill repute of both sexes, public sinners, were among his followers. This was an accusation against him. He loved them and was loved by them. They were loyal to him in life and in death. Women were among the principal witnesses to his message and to his resurrection. The Samaritan woman with five husbands and Mary Magdalene were among the first to evangelize others—to proclaim Jesus and his message. (Strangely enough, women could not preach in churches—at least till recent times.) His injunction against divorce was a defense of the rights of women, who could earlier be repudiated easily by their husbands. In that context this too was a progressive step. In all this Jesus was living up to his program of "liberating the captives and setting the downtrodden free."

In this sense it would be more valid to argue that Jesus was in favor of the liberation of women, rather than their domestication forever. He was far in advance of his day. If the church had continued his approach, the emancipation of women might have come much sooner in history. This is similar to the case of slavery. Jesus did not preach the immediate abolition of slavery as we understand it today. But his life and teaching were a rejection of the bases on which slavery was founded. The insistence on human dignity, on authority as service, on personal freedom, were quite contrary to the practices and legitimations of slavery in Jewish and Roman society.

It is important that the churches recognize this radical stance of Jesus concerning women too. We can then draw our conclusions with a dynamic view of history and not merely argue for the selective continuance of the status quo of Jewish society or of some of the practices of Jesus. In any case, this is one of the aspects in which the Eucharist has to be renewed today.

If women are not accepted as equal persons before the Eucharist, in the long term the churches will perhaps suffer much more than the women. For it is not likely that adult women will tolerate male chauvinism even in the religious sphere for many more decades. This is, however, not just a question of opportunism for the churches, but a matter of justice to all persons.

Women are being gradually liberated from the hard lot which has been theirs for generations. Even the dangers and difficulties of child-bearing are being reduced. Almost everywhere in the world the processes of family planning are reducing the number of years when women have to stay at home looking after the children. They are gaining more control over their own bodies and the functions of reproduction. They can give much more of their time to work outside the homes. The home chores are being increasingly reduced due to scientific advances and the better preparation of husbands to share them.

Women claim equality in every sphere of life as a right. In this they are right. The very consciousness of being oppressed is a dynamic to liberative action. We can regard these as a process of maturation of humanity. Women and men are being better respected as persons. The liberation of women, well understood, is also an opportunity for the humanization of man. Man can thus be less an exploiter of others.

In all this what is to be the role of the churches? Are they

going to be in the vanguard of this process? Or will they be
an obstacle to be overcome? The attitude of the churches
toward the role of women concerning the Eucharist is important in this regard. It is also symbolic of the entire
attitude of Christians toward women.

THE EUCHARIST AND OPPRESSED PEOPLES

As mentioned earlier, the history of the Eucharist is one
of very close association with oppression. After Christianity became the religion of the Roman Empire, the celebration of the Eucharist was absorbed by the social establishment as a special expression of its triumph. It gave
divine legitimation to power. Prior to that, catacombs and
private houses were the meeting places of the eucharistic
community. The Christians lived a rather underground
existence, especially during times of persecution. With the
conversion of Christianity and the Roman Empire to each
other, the big imperial basilicas were made available to the
churches. Thus during feudal times the lords of the manors
had their own churches. The ecclesiastical and civil lords
were closely linked in relationships of power and wealth.

There were naturally occasional conflicts between the
secular and religious powers; but the millennium of
feudalism was one in which by and large the power elite of
the church was on the side of the feudal nobles and kings.
It is important that this be remembered and reflected on
when we try to understand this tradition of the Eucharist
as subservient to power. It is only a few centuries ago that
Europe left feudalism behind. And what are a few centuries for those who think of "eternal Rome" and its mission to rule the Christian world? Medieval Christianity
tried to evolve some social norms concerning the just ruler,
just price, and fair wages. These were good and useful. But
there was no idea of changing the relationships of domination and dependence that feudalism implied. Today we
should not blame the past. But neither can we afford to
ignore it; for it lives with us as a permanent legacy. We

have to ask ourselves how the church was able to integrate itself and the Eucharist within feudalism. This implied a fundamental acceptance of the social system with its good and bad. Further, it meant in practice that the powerful in the church were able to benefit from the operation of the system. They found a sacral niche within the feudal hierarchy of power and privilege. A reflection on this can be a lesson for us concerning alliances between power and the eucharistic celebration in our times.

We referred earlier to the intimate connection between the Eucharist and the colonial expansion of Europe. Here too it is enlightening to ask ourselves how and why it was possible for the Christian conscience to be so conditioned that the celebration of the Eucharist could go hand in hand with history's worst plunder and genocide. It is the peoples who have suffered such oppression who are able to understand the heinousness of these crimes. Whereas Jesus gave his life for others, and the Eucharist is a memorial of that self-sacrifice, in the colonial expansion the roles were reversed. The "Christians" were the robbers and plunderers. They murdered in the name of the expansion of western civilization and of the religion of Christ. Entire populations and civilizations were wiped out from the face of the earth. The pope in Rome, who is considered the guardian of the eucharistic message and mystique, presided over this division of the then known world between the two major Catholic powers of the day: Spain and Portugal.

We are not repeating these things to retell their gruesome details. We wish, however, that the lessons of history be learned. We see that at each phase the eucharistic community was in the main oblivious to its obligation of love of neighbor. Rather, we should say more. The Christian community had even developed a theology and a spirituality that legitimized this cruel phase of European history. The authorities of the church who claimed to be God's special representatives and Christ's vicars did not really side with the people who were being exterminated. A few voices of protest were heard here and there. But these were exceptions. They were marginal to the main thrust of the "holy people of God." They were "eccentrics" who tried to identify with the oppressed. In fact they were even considered disobedient children who had to be watched by the local church and Christian civil rulers, so that the most worthy cause of the expansion of the kingdom of Christ might not be impeded.

The tragedy is that the peoples who have suffered thus either are no more as a people, or are unable to communicate their thinking to the church powers. We have to ask ourselves how theology was evolved in that day. How did theologians come to support such exploitation and suppress dissent? Why were the groans and squeals of the oppressed millions unable to penetrate to the ears and hearts of the successors of the apostles? Even more important is to ask ourselves whether or not the system has yet changed within the church. Is theology evolved very differently in the centers of church power? Do they have experience of suffering oppression?

An important theological conclusion is that when the "controllers" of theology and church discipline have no live experience of oppression, they are not likely to understand or even listen to the cries of the oppressed masses. Further, where the power elite of the church is ensconced within the exploiting group, they are likely to develop a theology which is in effect an ideology of conquest and domination. For this would suit their own interests. We are saying this as a conclusion of historical experience, and not as an ideological conclusion. It is a pity that many European thinkers and church authorities do not reflect adequately on this aspect of the history of theology and of church discipline. We have still to await a history of the church written from the point of view of the oppressed and marginated peoples of the world. Instead we have generally church histories written by the victors in the process of western expansion. The intercommunication between secular events and the ecclesiastical adaptations to them are not critically examined.

An important conclusion is that where ecclesiastical authorities and lawmakers are part of the ruling social establishment, the church law itself tends to be corrupted in favor of the powerful. Then the eucharistic norms are made to fit into the needs of an exploiting system. Another way of saying this is to ask: Who makes the church laws? Who decides the theology that is considered orthodox by church authorities? Ever since the Constantinian compromise, the oppressed have generally been at the receiving end of theology and spirituality. Even today, how far can workers influence the theology of Canterbury, Geneva, New York, Rome, or for that matter even Moscow? Where are the women theologians—except at the margins of churches, if they are present at all? The youth are not accepted as initiators and much less as determinants of theological thought.

Perhaps even more significant is the fact that the peoples of Asia, Africa, and Latin America have not been listened to in this historical process. It is not enough to have a few yellow, brown, or black faces in the ecclesiastical high courts. The voices of the oppressed masses, their sufferings and experiences, must be the subject matter of theology and spirituality. The Eucharist must take into account what is happening to these peoples and the causes of their worsening situations. We can at least hope that these considerations will make the present lawgivers of churches a little less cocksure of themselves. They should reflect on the situation that, for thousands of years, they and their predecessors have been on the exploiting side of history. This might have a salutary effect on them. They may then begin to question their present assumptions. They may not then come to conclusions so facilely. If ever they really suffer with the oppressed they may be able to give a new direction to the eucharistic practices too.

A repentant meditation on the colossal insensitivity of the eucharistic communities and especially of their lawgivers to plunder, enslavement, and murder by Christians may be the beginning of wisdom for the eucharistic groups of today. There was a certain repentance in the attitude of Vatican Council II toward the other Christians and the modern world of Western Europe and North America. This was salutary. It was a sign of hope. But it should only be a beginning. For there is much more for which the churches have to repent. This is especially true with reference to the working classes of the world and the peoples of Latin America, Asia, and Africa.

The Eucharist is in captivity. It is dominated by persons who do not experience oppression in their own selves. Even within the poor countries, the church leaders generally belong to and side with the affluent elite. The Eucharist will not be liberated to be true to its mission so long as the churches are captive within the world's power establishments. The eucharist has to be liberative; it should lead to sharing and genuine love. But in its social impact it fails to do so. It has been interpreted conservatively, rigidly, and formally. If, on the other hand, it were to become the ferment of contemporary Christianity, the churches would change radically. It is when Christians make a fundamental option against oppression, and struggle against it, that the Eucharist itself will be liberated. Already this is happening among certain groups committed to integral human liberation in the perspective of Jesus Christ.

Even with reference to interchurch ecumenism this is an important consideration. The Christian churches have differed and divided over their eucharistic teaching and practices also. But the more important point for the future getting together of the churches is not the exact doctrinal resolution of their divergences concerning the Eucharist or other issues of dogma. It is the option of the churches concerning the present struggle against oppression all over the world that will be the dividing line. Perhaps the churches as a whole will not make such options. They have not been able to express themselves unequivocally even about the Vietnam war or apartheid. Those who opt to struggle with the oppressed, the weak, the excluded, and the marginalized will be on one side, whatever their church denomination. Today the major division among Christians cuts across the frontiers of churches. Communion in the liberation struggle is increasingly becoming a more uniting factor than affiliation to ecclesiastical groups. When these issues are taken seriously communion within the same church becomes difficult unless it involves at least a desire for human liberation from oppression. Interclass communion is likely to be increasingly under question.

These are issues which Christians and the churches have to face in the coming years. Ecumenism in the sense of exchange of pulpits, visits by church leaders to each other, and beating of breasts for the evils of the Reformation will soon achieve its limited objectives. Repentence by Christians together for their whole historical complicity in the exploitation of the oppressed nations, classes, and sex is a more urgent and deeper requirement. As it takes place the Eucharist will be progressively liberated. The Eucharist, well celebrated, can also help raise this new consciousness and sensitivity among followers of Jesus Christ of all denominations.

Chapter VI

Youth and the Eucharist

The attitude of youth toward the Eucharist has much relevance for the future of the Eucharist and of the church. For this we can reflect on their attitude toward the Mass, the other eucharistic devotions, and the priesthood. Youth vary a great deal in different countries and within each country. They differ according to their sex, family background, urban and rural character, education, social options, and the like. Yet we can see certain characteristics that are common to youth of our time. We can then ask ourselves whether the Eucharist as it is celebrated today meets their needs and aspirations. The almost universal decrease in the vocations to the priesthood (and the religious life) is an indication that youth are not so attracted to this state of life as young persons were in the past generations. This is a sort of protest by youth. They are indirectly telling the church that they are not so much in favor of the priesthood—at least as it is presently conceived in the church. Does this mean that they are less generous than in the past? Or is it that the priesthood has less meaning today?

THE VALUES THAT YOUTH SEEK

We can try to discern the positive values in the aspirations of youth today. It goes without saying that among youth there is a big gap between aspiration and realization, between desire and implementation. However, it is useful to note the differences in aspirations between present-day youth and those of older generations. The values that modern youth seek may be summarized in relation to the following desires.

Authenticity

Modern youth lay greater stress on frankness, openness, and honesty. They are tired of dishonesty, duplicity, and hypocrisy, which they see around them, especially in adult society. They are sensitive to the prevalence of double standards in people—for example, between thought and action, speech and performance, public role and private activity, prayer and work, theory and practice. They are unsympathetic to mere outward protestation of reforms without any genuine change in real life.

Freedom

Modern youth value freedom much more than the youth of previous generations. They want autonomy with self-determination. They also demand and take freedom in many more areas of life than the youth of the past. They are aware that youth are an important sector of modern society, and that their countries depend on them for defense, especially in times of war and other difficulties. They are also conscious that their knowledge of world affairs and of science and technology is often more up to date than that of their parents. Many of the attitudes of present-day youth flow from such an awareness of their numbers, their education, and their sense of frustration with the values that prevail in adult society.

The youth want freedom in organization of their own lives—their leisure, their social life, their relations with each other, their studies, choice of career, sex and marriage, and so forth. The desire for freedom expresses itself in a demand for dialogue, participation, and creativity. They do not like to be dictated to. They want to be consulted, even if they will eventually accept the decision of elders. They want their point of view to be heard. For they are not sure that the older generation or authority has all the right answers. They have seen so many evil and cruel things being done in the name of authority, experience, nationalism, and even God. They are prepared to experiment in their own lives rather than merely accept taboos and inhibitions of previous generations. They appreciate originality and innovation rather than mere continuance of an unsatisfactory status quo. They do not mind being unconventional. They tend to build their own culture within their peer groups. They are thus able to withstand the social pressures toward conformism. They are prepared to learn by doing, even by making mistakes. They dislike a paternalism, however benevolent, that denies them the chance to grow, and to be themselves.

Justice

Youth today has a greater awareness of and concern for justice than perhaps ever in the past. They are particularly sensitive to the needs of social justice—at the level of local communities, nations, states, and the world at large. They want more respect for the human person and for his or her rights. They are more aware of the communitarian aspect of justice. They see the absence of effective sharing despite protestations of good will, aid, and charity by the affluent. They instinctively want real fellowship among persons and peoples. They are generally forced to enter the "system" as there are few viable alternatives. This leads to an alienation within their own being. The better spirits among them retain this inner dissatisfaction even when they have to work within an exploitative system and profit from it. All this makes also for a crisis of identity and values within them. They feel powerless to change the system; yet often inwardly they cannot accept it. Those disadvantaged by it feel its terrible oppression in unemployment, poverty, and malnutrition. They feel their powerlessness even more poignantly.

The media of communications make them aware that the world has the means to remedy such problems as malnutrition and hunger almost overnight if only the people of the world were prepared to share their goods with those in need. While the older generation take such situations for granted and even find excuses for justifying and maintaining the inequalities, the youth are inclined to rebel against them. In the process they question the entire ideological and organizational apparatus that has grown up with and defends these injustices.

These situations lead youth to a point of questioning the ideologies to which adult groups adhere and according to which the world is divided into rival and warring camps. The fundamentals of these "isms" are questioned insofar as they do not relate to integral human needs and cause unhappiness and divisions. Thus there is a certain skepticism and indifference toward thinking and ideologies such as capitalism, communism, nationalism, racism, Catholicism, and so forth. Youth want actions that are related to problems and not mere ideological postures for their own sake.

They are disenchanted with such phrases as "making the world safe for democracy," "building socialism," "saving souls," and so forth. They do not trust stances in favor of "law and order" or a mere preaching of "peace" that does not take into account the permanent violence that exists under the umbrella of "law and order" and favoritism. They do not believe in the paternalism of authorities who do not want real change. They are skeptical about the puritanism of a sexual morality that coexists with exploitation of a socio-economic type.

All these make youth distrust adult institutions, attitudes, stances, and even values. Some come to the point of no longer believing in them, at least until they see concrete results. Delay concerning practical action is regarded as a sign of unwillingness to act. They want quick action, for they are fed up with the "wait and see" prudent policies of the "establishment." There is a certain cult of immediacy—action here and now is more valid than promises of future action.

Relevance

Youth want thought and action to relate to real problems, and that at their deeper levels, instead of merely taking things for granted. Since they are aware of the inadequacies of many aspects of contemporary society they want study and action that has a realistic relationship to them.

They are afraid that one of the causes of the maintenance of an unjust status quo is the irrelevance of many of the lines of action undertaken by sincere groups. They do not see justification in routine, rules, organizations, and institutions merely because they exist or were prestigious in the public mind earlier. The question they constantly ask is, What is the relevance of those to our society today? Whom do they serve? Do they buttress privilege under the shibboleth of service?

In this sense they seem to be anti-institutionalist. They question the existing structures of power and organization, be they in the Pentagon, Kremlin, or Vatican. Many adults find it difficult to understand this quest of relevance of the youth. It is a desire for the reform of structures—even when it takes the form of an anarchical attitude toward existing institutions and structures. They want institutions and rules to have meaning for their lives and values. This is a questioning of mere formalism, traditionalism, or conventionalism which an earlier generation may have taken for granted.

Fellowship

The desire for togetherness is stronger in many youth than even among adults today. This is linked to their desire for freedom and for sharing. The gap between them and their elders makes the need to be with one's peer groups even greater. The search for meaning in life and for the identity of self is also better expressed within the youth groups. Here they can be more unconventional. They can give vent to their desire for experimentation. They want to experience life for themselves. They feel they can work out norms of relationships on their own level. They do not have much confidence in the codes of conduct imposed by elders, but often not observed by the lawmakers themselves. The quest for authenticity, freedom, and sharing takes place within the youth groups. Sometimes these too have their conflicts and inconsistencies, as is to be expected, for they too are not exempt from the general human weaknesses.

The relationships between the two sexes are much less restrained than was the case among the youth of an earlier generation. The opportunities of meeting normally and freely are more frequent even in societies which were traditionally more inhibitive. The anonymity of city life facilitates such mixing. These pose challenges to youth which they wish to try to solve on their own in the context of modern society. The sense of male domination or female inferiority is less strong among the young people of the present generation almost everywhere in the world.

We can thus see trends in different directions such as the youth contestation of society, the dropouts and hippies, gangsters, and also the new religious cults of the "Jesus Revolution," Hari Krishna, and others, particularly in the more affluent western capitalist countries. In the Asian, African, and Latin American situations some youth experience fellowship more deeply in their participation in the liberation struggles of their peoples, especially against the dictatorial rulers and foreign exploiters. This togetherness is expressed across national frontiers too, as when youth meet as volunteers, students, or tourists in foreign countries. They become friends more easily. Music and dance are a universal language in which all can participate. All these different and divergent trends indicate a greater and more conscious search for fellowship among youth who feel that they must make their own future.

Honesty in Religion

Religion is also somewhat suspect by youth, unless its adherents genuinely inspire relevant action, especially toward justice. They question the meaning and value of religious ideologies, ritual, prayers, organizations, institutions, power systems, and even the ultimate sanctions of afterlife. God himself is judged by such criteria. Or rather, they doubt the existence of a God created in the image of many "believers" who are indifferent to human problems.

This is not so much because they do not want an ideology, religion, authority, or institution; but they fail to see its usefulness as presently articulated or exercised. They are not so much irreligious as averse to a religion that seems to them more formalist than genuine, more conventional than sincere. They favor an open, honest, sincere, authentic religion that commits itself seriously to human values, cost what it may even to the religious institutions themselves.

They are not so enamored of the type of religiosity of the past that did not concern itself effectively with the needs and rights of others. They are not so concerned with a stress on "orthodoxy"—or what is called correctness of doctrine. For they see that churches have fought each other for centuries in the name of their relative orthodoxies and divine rights to teach others. They are more concerned with impact on real life in terms of the values of the religions—or "orthopraxis." Praxis, or practical action, is more important than beautiful theories. Prayer itself is questioned in relation to its impact on the life of those who pray and on their relationships with others.

The youth have been evolving this mentality over a period of years. A decade ago we remarked these trends. This means that in many countries persons below thirty or thirty-five years of age would tend to have opinions similar to those mentioned above. Or at least they might have entertained them for a period of their lives, even if the "system" has since taught them other lessons. All the same they are in a way marked for life by such a stage in their thinking.

It will not be difficult to see how these characteristics of modern youth can have a relationship to the Eucharist. The rigid control over the liturgy by the church authorities seems to go quite contrary to these youthful inspirations. Vatican II tries to meet them by stress on dialogue and participation. Yet we are far from responding to these aspirations.

Let us now look more specifically at the youth in Asian countries.

SOME CHARACTERISTICS OF ASIAN YOUTH

From a consideration of the situation in which the youth in Asia are placed we can see certain aspects which are more special to them—in addition to problems which are common to their age and the modern times.

In the West youth unrest is a byproduct of affluence. The manifestations like hippyism are possible only because of the high standard of living of families of the youth. In Asia youth unrest is a consequence of the poverty of the countries and the families. Its manifestations are less glamorous but more deeply radical. The very poverty makes for the apathy of the vast majority. In the West, the affluence of the system conditions many to conformism. The generation gap is perhaps wider in Asia, as the older generation is often less school-educated than their children and the differences between the old and the new world ethos are greater in Asia.

Many youth in the free-enterprise countries of Asia are condemned to chronic unemployment. Sri Lanka has about one million unemployed out of a total population of about 13.5 million. India is reckoned to have about 35 million unemployed. From decade to decade the situation seems to worsen in the free-enterprise countries. Unemployment results in the youth losing respect for themselves. They are disgusted with a social system that is incapable of making use of their creative activity. Some take to crime as a way out. Girls become prostitutes, especially in places where foreigners are numerous, such as Bangkok, Hong Kong, and Saigon during the war. Thus human beings are degraded. They are denied a sense of purpose and usefulness. Through no fault of their own they have to spend many of their young adult years as a burden to their families and to society. This leads to a deep-seated sense of frustration. Many youth are dissatisfied with the older generation even when it is composed of persons who worked in movements for political independence. They are discontented with the type of education which does not open opportunities for employment to them. The nepotism, opportunism, hypocrisy, and corruption so rampant in public life, especially among the nation's ruling elite, leads them to a sense of helpless disgust with the entire social framework.

Among Asian youth there is a greater awareness of economic and cultural domination by foreign powers and the local elite, and a preparedness for more radical reforms or even violent revolution as a way out of the present situation. They are disillusioned with mere ideologies —either of the right or of the left. They want practical solutions and honest leaders. They do not want to be pawns in the power struggles of political parties or of East and West in the world.

In Asia the youth are quite isolated as a group. They stand alone in society; numerous, but powerless; idealistic but incapable of implementing their desires. The search among youth here is not only for personal identity but also for national identity. This is quite pronounced in Hong Kong, Taiwan, and Singapore, where identity problems are paramount. It is also a deep-seated concern in India —what is the nation, where is it going?—in Indonesia, which has only recently been brought together to form a nation, thanks particularly to Sukarno and his choice of Basha Indonesia; in the Philippines, which is seeking its soul and liberation from martial law; in

Malaysia, trying to resolve its sensitive issues of race and religion. This problem of identity and ideology is quite acute in the two Koreas, in Vietnam, Cambodia, Laos, Pakistan, and Bangladesh. Burma is going its hard way to Burmese socialism in isolation and privation, but with a sense of rediscovered self-esteem and pride in its efforts. Likewise the other countries.

Asian youth are facing within themselves the problem of cultural identity. What are we? is a question they feel within themselves—Chinese or western? Indian in tradition or modern in attitudes? How are we to reconcile the ancient and the modern? The national and the modernizing trends from abroad? Traditional morality and the freer relations among the sexes which the cities and universities foster? Secularization and religious beliefs? Reverential awe of parents and freedom? Theirs is a problem of selfhood, self-expression, and self-realization.

In spite of all these problems and disabilities Asian youth have a profound sense of optimism, for they have a conviction that the future belongs to them. This is both with reference to the adults whom they will one day bury and the world establishment, which is antagonistic toward them. They hope some day to overthrow it too.

The sense of justice among Asian youth is born of an experience of personal suffering or injustice. Their desire for liberation bears within it an eschatological yearning for establishing a better community of humankind on this earth.

For Asian youth in general Christianity is not merely not so relevant to their problems, as western youth may think, but also alien to their countries. They generally regard Christianity as allied to the enemies of their nation and the exploiters of the poor. The youthful attitude of alienation from religion takes, therefore, a special form with reference to Christianity.

It is necessary, however, to remember that Asian youth, like all human beings, are also subject to the same human weakness, inconsistencies, and sinfulness. They too tend to choose easily the path of least resistance. However, in a reflection on the role of religions concerning youth, these considerations may be helpful.

Asian youth see that the socialist countries of their continent have been able to resolve the problems of food, unemployment, inflation, and national identity within the short space of two decades. On the other hand, the situation in the free-enterprise countries has worsened in the meantime. Even political freedom has been suppressed in many free-enterprise countries of Asia. This contrast poses ideological problems concerning the type of society they would like to opt for. This in turn is related to their attitude toward their religions, for the religions have often been antisocialist and anti-Marxist.

THE INADEQUACY OF THE CHURCH'S RESPONSE

Having seen who the Asian youth are, their problems and preoccupations and the values they seek, we can ask ourselves how the Eucharist has related to them in the past. This can help us take orientations for the future insofar as we wish to respond seriously as disciples of Jesus Christ to the demands of Asian youth today.

When we consider the values that modern youth cherish we can see why the Eucharist as traditionally celebrated has so little appeal to them. Whereas they appreciate spontaneity and freedom, the Eucharist had a rigidity that left little space for change. Instead of an authentic spiritual experience there was a formalist ceremony which all believers were obliged to attend once a week under pain of mortal sin. The teaching is that mortal sin is an alienation from God, and is punishable with eternal hellfire. Sunday attendance regularized this relationship with God. We have mentioned elsewhere how the Eucharist had little actual impact on social justice. Instead of helping build human community and fellowship it tended to legitimize the inequalities of society. All these meant that it was difficult to see an objective honesty in the eucharistic worship. The case of Ananias and Sapphira, who wanted to join the community of early Christians, who had all things in common, while keeping a part of the proceeds of their property for themselves, has some relevance today also. What is really the effect of the protestations of sharing the common table in fellowship?

Vatican Council II (1962–65) made very important changes in the liturgy of the Catholic church. It encouraged the active participation of all present at a eucharistic celebration. It made provision for the reform of the liturgy. The Mass was subsequently simplified. The Scripture readings were more systematically chosen. The celebration of the feasts of numerous saints was rationalized. The use of Latin was made optional. The vernacular was accepted as a language for celebration. Concelebration was encouraged. Openness to the culture and traditions of nonwestern peoples was considered feasible and encouraged with cautions.

These are the fruits of the liturgical revival, especially in Europe in the decades prior to Vatican Council II. But the Constitution on the Liturgy left the discretion of deciding liturgical issues with the hierarchy, the bishops and the Holy See.

The council held that "liturgical services are not private functions, but are celebrations of the church, which is the 'sacrament of unity,' namely the holy people united and ordered under their bishops" (no. 26). The council was still far from considering the liturgy in its aspect of active and effective participation in the liberative action of Jesus. This aspect of theology had not yet been developed in the church. The social dimension of the mission of Jesus is hardly seen in the Constitution on the Liturgy, which was the first definitive text of that council.

By the end of the council in 1965 the thinking of the council fathers on social issues was clearer, as can be seen in the Pastoral Constitution on the Church in the Modern World. But even here we are still a long way from understanding Jesus of Nazareth as a liberator of oppressed peoples, which understanding is somewhat widespread today in Asia, Africa, and especially Latin America. If the Constitution on the Liturgy had been drafted in 1965 at the end of the council, it would have been quite different. For by 1965 the council had acquired a certain dynamism of its own and the North American, Latin American, and Afro-Asian bishops were then beginning to awaken to their role and responsibility in the church.

Hence the liturgical changes of the past fifteen years have not adequately related to the aspiration of youth, especially of Asia, Africa, and Latin America. Euro-American youth found some leeway for self-expression for their concerns where the hierarchies were more liberal-minded. In other places, such as Holland, they took the initiative along with friendly priests. But the bulk of the church moved slowly concerning an active youth partici-pation in the liturgy. In some places there was a tug-of-war between the keen youth and rather conservative clergy and hierarchy. The deep concerns of youth could hardly find room for expression in a Sunday parish Mass. Occa-sionally there were youth Masses—but these were more of a cultural phenomenon with youth music and style of ex-pression. They seldom led to committed action. In the Uni-ted States the youth contestation concerning race, pov-erty, and the Vietnam war found some articulation in small group liturgies. But seldom did the anti-Vietnam war movement find inspiration and expression in the liturgies approved by the hierarchies.

The demands of youth in Asia are far more radical than those of their counterparts in Europe and North America. Here the youth face daily frustrations under a crushing socioeconomic system. Many among them want radical social change. All ask for food, work, houses, and social justice. Here the struggle for social justice is not a mere "corporal work of mercy." It is the fight for life itself. In Asia a spirituality that does not relate creatively to this situation is not only suspect, it can even be harmful. There can be no meaningful question here of separating "inter-nal" and "spiritual" sanctity from social commitment.

The liturgy of the churches has, so far, largely failed to relate to the urgent problems of the youth of Asia. This is not to ignore that some efforts have been made here and there. The problem is that the basic thrust is absent. There is a slight tinkering about issues of society, a minimal openness to other religions and occasional concessions to youth aspirations. But by and large the more dynamic youth of Asia have to move to other groups for motivation and sustenance in their life struggles. The incapability of Christianity to dialogue meaningfully with socialism and Marxism in Asia is another serious drawback. About half of Asia is under Marxist powers. In the other half, Marxist groups are very important forces either in official opposition parties or underground. Socialism is increasingly being accepted in Asia and Africa as the only feasible alternative to the present ills of the masses. Yet the Eucharist remains still substantially under the control of persons who are, in fact, of a capitalist frame of mind —even though they may well purport to be ideologically neutral.

This question is now posed in the Latin countries of Europe also. For Eurocommunism is gaining ground in Italy, France, Spain, Portugal, and parts of Belgium. The Catholic church has here a serious problem on its hands. It cannot for long outlaw the adherents of these trends, or even turn a blind eye to them. They are too numerous and too politically active to be ignored. Perhaps in having to respond to them the western churches might understand something of the anguish of the youth of Asia, Africa, and Latin America. Or will the church change only when it is too late—when the more radical youth have quit the eucharistic table for its want of meaning, community, freedom, authenticity, and relevant commitment to justice? How long will the church take to learn its lessons in Asia? Or has it first to die to its present forms in order that it may live in a more evangelical way?

The Eucharist has the capacity of also challenging youth toward a greater sense of community and commitment.

Youth all over the world are also tempted to be selfish, opportunist, and careerist. The temptation to obtain the favors of the powerful companies, governments, or groups is a constant danger for them. Those who rise up the ladder of wealth and power easily forget the others. The attraction of consumerism and satisfying oneself first is as much a pitfall for the elitist youth of the poor countries as it is for their fellow youth in the rich north. Both capitalist and socialist countries can hold these carrots to the youth; for thereby their natural generosity can be domesticated in the service of the ruling establishments. On the other hand, the poorer and less influential youth may be inclined to be discouraged and pessimistic.

To all these categories of youth the Eucharist meaningfully celebrated can be a help, a motivating influence, and a sustaining force. It can interpret to them the spiritual meaning of concern for others even to the disadvantage of self. Jesus gave himself for others. This is the noblest and final gift that anyone can offer for others. This is also the best worship of the Father, as Jesus has shown us in his Last Supper and death. It is also thanksgiving to God for our own lives and his graces—the supreme gift of the return of our lives to him in the service of others. It is sometimes more difficult to live and struggle in this cause of integral human liberation than even to die instantaneously at the hands of oppressors as a martyr. For the Eucharist to be such a challenge to youth the adult church itself would have first to lead the way in such commitment.

Chapter VII

The Eucharist and Socialism

Since the Eucharist has been adopted to subserve the feudal, capitalist, and imperialist societies, the relationship between the eucharistic communities and socialist societies has been rather strained and even positively antagonistic. Socialism in the past hundred years has been mainly inspired by Marxism. There has been a severe conflict between Christianity and Marxism during this period, till very recent years. Christian churches, especially the Catholic church, have excommunicated Communists. For their part the communist societies have placed severe restrictions on Christians. We can remember Pope Pius XII excommunicating the rulers of Hungary who imprisoned Cardinal Mindzenty. However, recently Pope Paul VI received Janoz Kadar, the secretary of the Hungarian Communist Party, at the Vatican. The pope and the communist ruler emphasized the need of friendly relationships between the socialist state and the Catholic church. Hence over the years there has been a significant evolution in the relationships between these two important groups in today's world.

COMMON ROOTS

In a sense the Eucharist and the inspiration toward socialism are intimately linked in their historical sources. The first eucharistic communities were ones that encouraged a socialistic form of living. This related only to the distribution of goods and not the mode of production; yet it has been a source of inspiration for much radical social thought of later periods.

For the early Christians the ceremony of the breaking of bread—the Eucharist—was intimately connected with the sharing of bread. It was not a mere formalist ceremonial. The Eucharist signified sharing. It also brought about what it signified. The rite and the reality were intimately linked. The symbol was for real. They tried to practice what they professed. We have seen how the early Christian groups shared what they had so that there was no one in need.

For Jesus, too, the Last Supper, the first and inaugural Eucharist, was closely associated with his self-giving. He gave bread and wine, saying, "This is my body," "This is my blood." This was not merely a symbol, rite, or ceremony. He said that he was giving himself—his life—for his people. He then gave a new commandment: "Love one another; as I have loved you, so you are to love one another. If there is this love among you, then all will know you are my disciples." He enjoined them to love even their enemies. For Jesus the Eucharist was a supreme act of concern for others, of sharing, of community. His own body was being broken and his blood shed. He was not merely giving bread, or a bit of property; he gave his life for the liberation of others. He was killed because he championed justice, the truth, the poor, and the exploited. He took an unflinching stand against injustice, deception, and the exploitation of the poor and the weak. Like the bread that he broke and gave his disciples, his body was to be broken, scourged, and crucified by the powerful of the day and their agents. The Eucharist signifies this being broken for others. His sacrifice was the supreme one of offering his blood up to the last drop for his cause. He endured immense and intense suffering of mind and body to bear witness to his message that God is love, and love demands justice and truth.

If the Eucharist is *lived* by those who celebrate it, sharing will have to be practiced by them. This is a primary

THE EUCHARIST AND SOCIALISM

requisite of the eucharistic community or church. Since
love is to be for all, sharing must also be with all others too.
The Eucharist is anti-individualistic. It is not compatible
with a philosophy of selfish profit maximization for persons or private groups. The Eucharist cannot really coex-
ist with vast gaps of wealth and misery. This would be a
mockery of Jesus and his life message.

The Eucharist does not indicate a mode of production or
a form of social organization. But it does demand effective
sharing in freedom. In this sense the Eucharist relates
better to an effectively socialistic society. No one should be
in need. All things should be for the needs of all. Self-
sacrifice must be prior to selfishness and acquisition of
things for oneself. Since the Eucharist demands that we
live for others, how much more does it demand that we
should work for them. If our life has to be given for others
in truth, love, and justice, how much more does it demand
that property be for all. Thus the Eucharist emphasizes
basic values which are closely related to the ideals and
priorities of a socialistic way of life.

The Eucharist and the profit maximization of capitalism
are incompatible. The Eucharist cannot be meaningfully
celebrated by persons who spend lavishly on themselves
—as in the first-class hotels, while others live off the dust-
bins close by. At least the Eucharist should impel them to
strive hard to change such a situation. Otherwise their
lives would be like that of the Pharisees and scribes whom
Jesus condemned categorically.

The Eucharistic Ideal and Marx's Vision

Karl Marx as a Jew knew of this tradition of expectation
of ultimate justice and joy. It was part of the messianism of
the Jewish people. The Jews have had a haunting yearning
for this promised land. It was a land of sharing but also of
plenty—a land flowing with milk and honey. Jesus gave a
deeper meaning to this expectation in the self-sacrificial
love of sharing. Marx gave another interpretation to this
tradition. He expressed the stage of ultimate blessedness

as the classless society. For him exploitation is humanity's sin. Exploitation is to be ended by revolution. Class struggle is the path to revolution. Dictatorship of the proletariat is the means to the establishment of socialism. The common ownership of the means of production, distribution, and exchange is the way to ensuring the needs of all. This form of socialism is to lead to the liberation of human persons from the alienations to which they are subjected under capitalism. Work would not alienate people, because they would receive its time value. Woman would be liberated from male dominance because she would be an equal partner in a society in which all work and all share its fruits. Culture would flourish without being commercialized as in the capitalist societies. All things will be in common, and no one will be in need. All can then sing the hymn of glory to a liberated humanity.

We can thus see a close connection between the eucharistic ideal and Karl Marx's vision of a classless society. Yet one believes in a God who is love, and the other is atheistic but posits the possibility of a high degree of unselfishness in human beings. While seeing the fundamental differences it is important for us to see the similarities and even the common historical roots of the two visions, the two aspirations for human liberation. Each is capable of being corrupted by human selfishness. Each needs constant purification. Thus while there are often sharp divergences between Christians and Marxists, there is also a very deep interconnection. This can be a basis for a meaningful dialogue between them. It can also help in a mutual self-purification. Marxism can teach Christians what the Eucharist must mean in the real world of class exploitation. Christians can recall Marxists to the ideal of the classless society in which human beings must all be respected in equality and freedom. Where Christians side with the powerful exploiting capitalist establishment, Marxism can have a prophetic role to remind Christians of their own values. On the other hand, when Marxists become the socio-political power elite, then Christianity can have the mission of recalling Marxists to their own ideals of human liberation.

Values of Socialism

Socialism has various forms. We can, however, see certain values which are implied in socialism. These constitute its appeal. Socialism is based on a respect for the human being, for all persons, whatever their age, sex, race, creed, or work. It seeks to ensure the basic needs of all. The means of production are to be owned in common. Production is to be for the benefit of all. The fruits of work are to be for all. Socialism seeks also to respect the dignity of the human person, safeguard his or her freedom, and provide the environment for the full moral and cultural fulfillment of each one in community. Socialism is egalitarian and communitarian. There are doubtless deficiencies in the different historical experiences of socialism. Human efforts are bound to fall short of such a high ideal. But the values and priorities of socialism are intrinsically better than the efforts to build societies based on private profit and individualism, for these are inherently antisocial and create much greater inequalities.

Socialism is, however, wider than Marxism. The eucharistic sharing can relate to all forms of socialism provided there is a genuine effort toward sharing in freedom. Even if the whole world becomes socialist, it will not fit into one single narrow socialistic mold. There will be differences even within socialism. Already there are several schools of Marxism itself—Mao's China is different from the Soviet Union; Yugoslavia's socialism differs from Mongolia's model. Western Europeans are thinking of a Eurocommunism in which socialism will respect the culture and religion of the peoples. Thus humanity will evolve. Socialism, and not capitalism, is undoubtedly the way of the future of humanity.

While people go ahead on this road, the followers of Jesus can find in the Eucharist inspiration for commitment to integral social justice. Insofar as their societies tend toward socialism, they too can help in building genuine communities of sharing and caring. But this will require a radical change in their lives, away from individualistic acquisition to "having all things in common," so that "no one is in need," as happened among the early Christians. The Eucharist must therefore be a dynamic of social change. Its social impact has to be revolutionary in societies where inequalities prevail. The Eucharist cannot be well celebrated without a respect for human persons. Hence it demands the championing of human rights. This is a challenge to Christians in socialistic societies also. For socialism can, in practice, lead to much abuse of power. It can be dictatorial. Then it does not really ensure equality or freedom. The eucharistic celebration is thus a permanent challenge to the followers of Jesus to try to build real human communities of effective sharing and unselfish love.

In this sense the eucharistic table prefigures the ultimate stage of human liberation, the realization of the kingdom of God on earth as in heaven. It is eschatological. It signifies the stage promised in the Scriptures when the lion and the lamb can lie together and share the same pasture; when every tear will be wiped from every eye; when God will be all-in-all. This is the Christian hope, the promised stage of human blessedness. This is also part of the Jewish tradition.

REAL-WORLD PARADOXES

In real life, however, the situation has been quite different. The eucharistic communities have in most countries been concerned with activities that did not help bring about effective long-term sharing based on changes in the structures of society. Marxist socialists, on the contrary, have been quite alive to the need of fundamental changes in the social relations.

Christians, when they meet in the parish liturgies, are usually interested in their own parochial concerns and charitable activities. It is surprising to see how much of parish life is geared toward charity, church buildings, educational activities, and fund raising for them. In certain countries the parish is a hub of such activities as festivals, fairs, tombola, bingo, sports clubs, and recreation rooms. Groups like the Ladies of Charity, Red Cross, Boy Scouts, and Girl Guides find inspiration and accommodation within church premises. The churches utilize the eucharistic gatherings to conscientize people about floods, earthquakes, and other emergencies.

Such social services carried out with much goodwill, but in a merely charitable manner, do not basically change the relationships between the exploiter and the exploited. Three hundred years of the activities of St. Vincent de Paul societies did not prevent "Christian" France from exploiting Africa or Indochina. Some social services are, in a way, dangerous. For they tranquilize the people of goodwill within an oppressive situation. The victims are placed on the dole and the exploiters are made benefactors, philanthropists, and "donor" countries. The paradox is heightened when an exploiting capitalist is made a papal knight and given a place of honor in solemn eucharistic ceremonies.

While eucharistic groups in capitalist countries have been largely involved in such irrelevancies or marginal assistance, the socialists and Marxists are usually busy around more fundamental issues. They help organize laborers into trade unions. They analyze social issues more critically and with a view to justice. They form themselves into political parties. They bring political pressure for land reform, for improving the conditions of the working classes. They combat imperialism and capitalism. They are often attacked by the well-to-do in society. Sometimes they have to go underground when repression takes a more violent form. Generally they campaign for the dignity of the human person, for the rights of women and of poor countries.

The paradox is that while the example of Jesus should make the eucharistic community a champion of social justice and a contestant of social evil, this happens very seldom; even then the official church leadership looks askance at it. On the other hand, Marxists have been regarded as committed to an ideology that is "intrinsically evil" with whom "those who would preserve Christian civilization from ruin cannot collaborate in any way" (see Pope Pius XI's encyclical *Divini Redemptoris*, 1936). It is, however, Marxists who have been in the vanguard of most of the movements for a radical economic and political liberation of the workers and poor nations. No major national liberation movement has succeeded in overthrowing colonialism and capitalism without the leadership of the Marxist parties. These are realities we cannot escape in this last quarter of the twentieth century.

The paradox is, however, not so one-sided. For we find that once Marxism is successful and establishes itself as a ruling power, it also tends to be dogmatic and authoritarian. The socialist countries have, over a period of time, resolved the basic problems of food, clothing, housing, and employment for their peoples. This is a very positive achievement. No poor capitalist or free-enterprise country has provided them for all their citizens. Yet we have to recognize the problems that remain within socialist countries too—especially those of human freedom, for example, the rights of free association, movement, speech, and publication. Once in power the revolutionaries of yesterday tend to become the new establishment. Hence the need of a permanent revolution or of cultural revolutions.

When they become more conscious of the social demands of the Gospel Christians tend to join the ranks of radical thinkers and activists. This has taken place in groups in Latin America, the United States, South Korea, the Philippines, Angola, Mozambique, and Western Europe. These are often marginal to the official church. When Marxism is the established power, the Christians are in some way radical contestants. Affirming a belief in God, the eucharistic community then becomes an alternative source of motivation, different from the atheism of the ruling communist parties.

Fidel Castro expressed this paradox succinctly in January 1968 in his closing speech for the Congress of Intellectuals:

Marxism has to grow, to stop being hidebound, to interpret with an objective and scientific spirit the realities of today, to behave like a revolutionary force and not like a pseudo-revolutionary Church. . . . These are paradoxes of history: Now, when we see sectors of the clergy becoming revolutionary forces, can we be resigned to see sectors of Marxism becoming ecclesiastical forces? The idea of a *critical Marxism*, as opposed to a *traditional Marxism* has now become quite routine in the Marxist camp (Quoted by Arturo Gaete, "Christians and Marxism: Pius XI to Paul VI," LADOC, USCC, Washington D.C., January 1974).

For our present purposes it is sufficient to note that the problems of the relationship between eucharistic groups and socialists is now quite a variegated one in a fast-evolving situation.

AN INESCAPABLE ENCOUNTER

Today the social evolution of the world has reached a position in which the encounter between Christianity and Marxism is both urgent and inescapable. Marxism is now a major protagonist in the struggle for the future of the world. It has both an ideology and a consequent complex of designs for economic, political, and social life. Marxism has spread over the globe faster than any ideology—other than, perhaps, capitalism. It triumphed in Russia only sixty years ago. Three decades ago communist regimes were set up in Eastern Europe, North Korea, and the People's Republic of China. The Cuban revolution was victorious by 1959. In Vietnam, Laos, and Cambodia it was Marxist-led forces that were able to withstand the might of the United States bombing and of half a million well-armed American soldiers. In many other Asian countries Marxism exercises influence in the search for a new social order. In certain nations Marxist parties are legally recognized political groups, for example, in India and Sri Lanka. In many other countries they are outlawed but influential underground, as in Indonesia, the Philippines, and Taiwan. In Africa many have turned to Marxism and indigenous kinds of socialism, as in Mozambique, Angola, Tanzania, and the liberation movements of Southern Africa.

In Latin America the Marxist parties have now become most serious competitors for national power. The success of the Cuban revolution and the failure of Allende in Chile have opened them to the need of more serious commitment. The very brutality of the right-wing dictatorships in Latin America is radicalizing more and more people toward militant socialist options. The meeting of Marxism and Christianity is already taking place within the active struggles and in the evolution of theological thought there. The Latin American theology of liberation accepts much of the Marxist social analysis. Yet it is fundamentally inspired by the radical biblical perspectives of liberation, as in the Exodus and in the life of Jesus Christ. The official churches are still wary of this theology; but sooner or later they will have to face the reality that the Latin American people want to understand Christianity in their own situation. Their emphasis on basic communities is cutting across the rigid hierarchical structures of parishes and other ecclesiastical organizations.

Levels of Encounter

Thus all over the world a meeting is taking place between Marxists and Christians, between socialist groups and eucharistic groups. Whereas a few decades ago these were mutually exclusive, today a cross-fertilization is taking place. The first level of encounter is generally in the field of *practical action*. For instance, in Sri Lanka today Marxists and believers of all religions work together in political parties, trade unions, mass media, and even inside the ruling cabinet. They meet on common human problems, though each one's thinking has an impact on one's perspectives.

A second level of meeting is *at the theoretical level.* Intellectuals all over the world are posing themselves questions concerning the nature of society, of religions, and ideologies. The rift between the U.S.S.R. and the People's Republic of China has meant that there is no single socialist homeland or Marxist orthodoxy. The rapprochement between the Eastern European socialist countries and the North Atlantic alliance of capitalist Western Europe and North America is raising further intellectual challenges to the traditional approaches of both Christians and Marxists. How far have these groups been right in thinking that divisions of faith or class were the main dividing lines of humanity? The detente between European East and West is bringing out more clearly the commonality of interests of the western powers and peoples, be they capitalist or socialist, Catholic, Orthodox, or Protestant. Their togetherness in the world system is affirming itself beyond ideologies and religions. Hence the whole intellectual framework of analysis is being requestioned by both Marxist and Christian thinkers.

A third level of dialogue is *institutional.* At the top levels of the Christian and Marxist establishments, there is a continuous effort at encounter. Thus the Vatican sends its emissaries to the Eastern European countries. The Soviet Union recently hosted the World Conference of Religions for Lasting Peace, Disarmament and Just Relations among Nations. The sixtieth anniversary of the October Revolution of 1917 paradoxically witnessed this large gathering of persons committed to religions from 107 countries of the world.

Contacts are taking place institutionally at the periphery and at grassroots levels too. Some Marxist parties are in contact with church groups. Some persons are Communists in their political options and eucharistic communicants in Christian churches. The growth of these contacts is also raising questions for both Marxist and

Christian groups. Sometimes the right hand of a church does not know, or ignores, what its left hand does. Recently, while the Holy Father was receiving the communist ruler of Hungary in special audience and the Vatican was represented as an Observer at the World Conference of Religions in Moscow, other Vatican curial bodies were active, working against communist influence among Christians, including the Prague-based Christian Peace Conference. The presence of the pope in Rome and the political pressures of the Vatican have not prevented Italians from electing a communist as mayor of Rome. The pope has since met the mayor in a cordial manner. This type of situation is becoming quite widespread in the world. In Italy, France, Spain, and Portugal many church leaders and Christians are now sympathetic to socialism and open to serious dialogue with Marxists. In Vietnam the Catholic hierarchy has motivated the Christians to cooperate in building socialism. Archbishop Nguyen Van Binh of Saigon has led in this in the South.

The Eucharist in Socialist Countries

In the countries of Eastern Europe where Marxism is the ideology of the state, the Sunday Eucharist was the maximum extent of religious organization permitted to Christians by the state. Over the years the areas of freedom have been somewhat extended. It is noteworthy that the Eucharist was able to maintain the continuity of the Christian tradition even in the U.S.S.R. In spite of sixty years of Marxist rule and atheistic propaganda, the churches continue to attract large numbers for their eucharistic services. In the socialist countries of Eastern Europe the resilience of Christians has been even greater.

In these countries the eucharistic services are ensured by a clergy that have had to adapt themselves to the socialist pattern of life. They have to depend on the support of the laity. The higher ecclesiastical leaders are, however, well provided, sometimes even in such a way as to be able to exercise their traditional hospitality in a lordly manner. The formation of priests is ensured by the sacrifice of the people and work of seminarians themselves. The experience of socialism has had a varying impact on the churches. Some Christians have remained rather conservative and unhappy with socialism. Their number is rapidly decreasing with the passage of years. Most Christians in Eastern Europe are now reconciled to the socialistic form of economy. Some of them are even close to the Marxist establishment; they tend to support the regime enthusiastically and without reserve, at least in public. This may be due to a conviction of its merits or even a measure of prudence. Among some others we see the beginnings of a new phase in which Christians are raising the issues of human rights within socialistic societies. Socialism has now reached a fair stage of affluence in Eastern Europe. Detente and the Helsinki Accord are giving the peoples of these countries greater possibilities of public pressure for more freedom or other rights. In some instances the church hierarchies have been with the people in their protests—as in the case of the workers in Poland. In any case the Christian communities have preserved their identity and continuity in very trying and novel circumstances. They have needed a good combination of discretion and valor to survive and even prosper spiritually during the years. Poland now sends missionaries to Africa.

These situations make the eucharistic celebration of greater significance in these countries. There is a likelihood that limits are placed on the extent to which the sermon can relate to social issues. However, the cult is the place of meeting of the masses of the people. It is one of the few spaces of encounter not planned by the state apparatus. Youth in these countries are showing a greater interest in religion, God, and transcendental values, as they find that economic security and materialism do not answer all their questions. This indeed is a strange verdict of human beings on an effort to wipe out the name of God and the problems of afterlife from the face of an entire

country during two generations. As these countries go
forward toward a greater democratization of their socialistic policies, the impact of the churches is likely to be
more marked.

The socialist countries try to retain religion within the
limits of cult and a hierarchical structure on the basis that
religion is a private affair. No church schools or lay apostolate or youth organizations are permitted. Religious orders have been dissolved or greatly reduced in numbers.
Many monasteries have been converted to other uses.
Training for priesthood has been made difficult. Publica-
tions are strictly controlled. Being a Christian is a disqual-
ification for important public offices, which are reserved
for members of the Communist party.

Sri Lanka

The churches and Marxist political parties in Sri Lanka
have gone through a significant evolution during the past
forty years. From the 1930s to the early 1950s the churches
were strongly anticommunist. This was perhaps the most
important determining element in the orientations of the
churches, especially of the Catholic church. The Catholic
leadership felt that it had a sacred duty to combat atheism.
In the general elections of 1947 and 1952, the Catholic
leadership clearly indicated to their followers that they
could not vote for a Marxist party. This was the time of the
excommunication of Communists. Since 1956 Marxists
have been cabinet ministers in almost every government.
The churches had to adapt themselves to this situation.

In the early 1960s the Marxist parties supported the
state takeover of denominational schools. The Christians
then felt that this would be a danger to their faith. They
feared that the state machinery would be used for the
indoctrination of children. But what happened was different. The state made the teaching of all religions compul-
sory in the socialized schools. Though there are certain
disadvantages in the present system, the teaching of religion is still a possibility even within the school. The school

takeover in a sense liberated the Christians to be less institutional and ghettoish.

During the second half of the sixties the Christians went through a rethinking that was collective though somewhat imperceptible. It was the post-Vatican II era. They were less wary of Marxism. Some were even in favor of socialism. In the election of 1970 some Christian areas supported the Centre-Left alliance of Mrs. Sirima Bandaranaike's Freedom Party and the Marxist parties. By this time Christian groups had begun to affirm themselves in favor of radical social change. In December 1970 the new government invited Pope Paul VI to Sri Lanka. He was warmly received by the prime minister and the entire cabinet, including the Marxist ministers. The pope celebrated the Eucharist at the international airport. The radical land reform and other socialistic measures of this government had the strong, though critical, support of many Christian groups.

In the 1977 general election campaign Marxism and religion were not real issues. Hardly anyone speaks of this today on the public platforms or in the mass media. All the political parties profess to be socialistic. We have now a position where assemblies of priests and laity invite all political parties to address them on their policies. There are divergences on policies among citizens. But we have now passed the point where it can be credibly argued that Christians cannot work with or within Marxist parties. This is a big change that reflects the overall worldwide shift of emphasis.

It can be said that today a substantial number of Christians and members of other religions in Sri Lanka favor a more socialistic policy to be worked out together by all socialist parties within a democratic framework. The Marxists, for their part, are discovering that religion is a far more deeprooted phenomenon than orthodox dialectical materialism might be wont to concede. Further, they are also coming to the conclusion that a multiparty system has certain important advantages that are absent in the one-party governments of many Marxist regimes. This confluence of trends, which is the result of Sri Lanka's own historical experience, has much to teach us. The churches have not yet consciously reflected on the implications of this evolution for their public worship and eucharistic practices.

Challenges for the Eucharist

The encounter with socialism is posing new and different challenges to the Eucharist. The Marxist analysis and action requires of Christians a response on social issues. Even if Christians are indifferent they are never neutral. The eucharistic communities have to recognize the existence and impact of class divisions in society. They can do so only with a greater weight being given to experience and the social sciences. Hence a traditional theology alone cannot help the church groups to meet this situation. The clash of interests of institutions and power blocs must be seen in their raw reality. They call for an option by the worshiping community.

When Marxism is in the opposition or underground the Christian solidarity with the oppressed requires an understanding of the cause for which they struggle. This means a critique of the operation of capitalism and of the remnants of feudalism in our societies. On the other hand, when Marxism is in power, the same solidarity with the oppressed has to see the types of oppression which a triumphant Marxist group can generate. For Marxism and socialism are not ultimate panaceas. They help resolve many basic problems, but still there is room for abuse of power and the growth of privilege.

The eucharistic community that is conformist under capitalism is also likely to be so under a new regime even if it is Marxist, for it would not have developed its critical insights and potentialities of dissent. On the other hand, those who give critical support to the establishment of socialist or Marxist regimes are more likely to be sensitive to the need of permanent vigilance and defense of human rights. When socialism is in power there is a greater need of intermediate institutions in a society to safeguard human rights. The former defenses of property and free enterprise largely disappear. Hence new agencies need to be developed if the state is not to be an overbearing monolithic power. In this situation the religious groups are a very important source of alternative motivation and organization. The challenge to the eucharistic groups is to be able to fulfill this function in an ongoing manner.

The churches have also the permanent mission of reminding humanity that socio-economic and political solutions are not the ultimate levels of the human search. They are important and essential. Yet beyond them we need deeper levels of acceptance, participation, and love. These can be witnessed to by persons and communities that believe in transcendental values. The message of Jesus in the Eucharist, sealed on Calvary, is an even deeper level of self-giving that shows a way for further human perfection within and beyond the practicable stages of a socialistic society. The Christian community has a meaning for human life at the deepest level of life, suffering, joy, death, and the hereafter. It has to keep alive this message in and through its commitment to human solidarity, especially with the oppressed. The fact that Marxism and socialism have not been able to replace or supplant the religions in their countries is an indication of the importance of these transcendental values for human life. The challenge for the Eucharist in such societies is to keep them alive in a dynamic tension between commitment to the real struggles of the people and pointing to the still deeper yearnings of the human person and community.

Chapter VIII

The Eucharist in Sri Lanka over the Centuries

Considerations discussed in the previous chapters point to the grave need of fundamental reorientations in the liturgical worship of Christians as well as in their overall approach to life as believers in the gospel of Jesus Christ. When such questions are discussed, a usual objection to change put forward by more conservative-minded persons is that "our people" are not ready for changes. It is said that Sri Lankan Christians, particularly Catholics, are simple, traditional, and conservative; that they have been so in the past and will continue to be like that in the future. Changes may be acceptable in a city like Colombo but not in the villages. Or they may be all right in far-off villages like Uva but not in Negombo—the little Rome. Such attitudes can be met even regarding fairly simple questions such as that of clerical dress.

We have to ask ourselves: Have the people always been so? Is it in the nature of ordinary people to be opposed to changes when they are needed? Do pressures for radical change come only from the top? Are the masses not capable of them? Why is it that people at a given time or place think and react in a particular way? Can it be due to the way they have been instructed and motivated by their leadership? In this a brief look at Sri Lankan church history can be quite instructive.

96

THE EUCHARIST
IN PORTUGUESE TIMES (1505–1656)

According to known records, the first Mass was celebrated in Sri Lanka in 1505 by the Franciscan missionary Frey Vincente, who accompanied Dom Lourenço de Almeida when his fleet strayed onto Sri Lankan shores. One of the conditions of the treaty negotiated between Dom Lourenço and Vira Parakrama Bahu VIII, the ruler of Kotte, included permission to build a chapel in Colombo near the Portuguese factory. In the early decades the priests served only as chaplains to the Portuguese settlement of merchants, soldiers, and sailors. One can therefore envisage the type of theology that would have been associated with such a mission and eucharistic service. The Franciscans who came with the merchants would not have had a refined sense of social justice, for they had to go along with the imperial advance of the Portuguese and console them in their needs. Evidently they could not question the overall goal of their expansion into these new lands. They had a theology of the Eucharist that had to do with the salvation of souls through conversion and the glory to God in prayer. But they could not think of the Mass as a continuation of the lifework of Christ in relation to human liberation. From the 1540s the conversion of the local population to Catholicism was taken up seriously by the Portuguese missionaries.

The Portuguese had much success in establishing the Christian faith in Sri Lanka. The expansive religious expression of the peoples of southern Europe responded to the religious sentiments of Sri Lankans. They built churches and established schools and colleges within their colonial territory. Social service was a hallmark of the Christians. We can gauge the success of their work from the record of the perseverance of the Catholics during 140 years of Dutch persecution, from 1656 to 1796.

While recognizing these strong points, it is not out of place to remark that Portuguese missionary methods, with the concept of priesthood and the Eucharist, were tainted by colonialism. To be Catholic meant becoming more or less Portuguese. The values of Sri Lankan Christians had to be akin to those of the Portuguese. The interests of the church were closely connected with those of the Portuguese state.

Other religions were not only not understood, but were even despised and attacked where the Portuguese were in power. Naturally the eucharistic services could not upset the arrangements made by the ruling power. The sermons had to conform to the interests of the Portuguese. The people had to learn a new type of worship, which implicitly gave a divine sanction to Portuguese rule. The liturgy was transplanted from Portugal.

The Portuguese missionaries do not seem to have ordained natives to the ranks of the priesthood, with the occasional exception of a person of royal blood. One of them, Don Juan, was ordained in Lisbon, and two princes were sent by Franciscans to Goa for the priesthood. The Mass was in Latin. Though some missionaries knew Sinhala, there is no record of translations of the Scriptures into Sinhala or Tamil. The instruction seems to have been oral. The Catholics seem to have had sufficient instruction to be steadfast in their faith even under conditions of persecution, as in Mannar and later in Dutch times.

At the time, the Portuguese were unable to distinguish, in practice, between the interests of Catholicism and those of the Portuguese regime. Since there was no native clergy, the active leadership of the Catholic community was in the hands of the foreigners—the Portuguese. When, a century later, the Dutch attacked the Portuguese for the trade of Sri Lanka, the Portuguese priests fought to the last against the Dutch. During the final seven-month siege of Colombo by the Dutch, the Catholic priests—Franciscans, Jesuits, Augustinians, and Dominicans—

combined the offering of the Eucharist with tending the sick and participating in the active defense of their fortress. S. G. Perera cites the valiant deed of one of them:

Towards the end of the fatal siege when men had fallen and the garrison [was] reduced, it became a matter of life and death to man the defences. The Jesuits as well as the other religious strove might and main to give the defenders every assistance. They shared their dangers, accompanied them in their sallies and stood by them at time of death. They carried arms and ammunition, to keep the scanty defenders well supplied, and when ammunition ran short it was the task of the religious to protect what remained of it at the risk of their lives. They took their turn at guarding and watching, and in time of assault they boldly took the posts of danger, without forgetting their foremost duty of assisting the fallen in the hour of death.

In such labours there fell the two Fathers Antonio Nunes and Manoel Velles. On 7 May, 1656, five days before the fall of the city, when the bastion of St. John was being scaled by the Dutch, Father Manoel Velles accompanied two soldiers to the fray and when they were slain he retreated with drawn sword. As they soon became masters of the post, some soldiers tried to renew the struggle. Having made their confession to Father Velles the party rushed against more than a hundred Hollanders. There fell Father Nunes, the Jesuit, a Pattern of Virtue, who signalized himself not only all along on the Bastion of St. John but also in other parts of the city, by encouraging the Soldiers, comforting the Sick and burying the Dead. He was shot at the Gate of the Bastion with a Musket-Ball, received afterwards a deep cut, and [was] at last slain by a hand grenade after he had killed several of the Enemy with his Musketoon. . . . During the long siege he was no less conspicuous for his charity and zeal for the salvation of souls than for the valour he displayed when occasion demanded. . . .

He was at the Bastion of St. John during the siege consoling and encouraging the soldiers by Mass, sermons and litanies (S. G. Perera, S.J., quoting Queyroz, in *The Jesuits in Ceylon*, Madura, 1941, pp. 125–26).

This quotation is given at length to enable an understanding of the intimate connection between the Portuguese and the Catholic religion, the priests and the soldiers, the Eucharist and their life-and-death struggle.

When the Portuguese surrendered to the Dutch, one of the clauses of the treaty of armistice was that all the clergy would be allowed to leave the country. For they were all Portuguese and hence enemies of the new regime. It was at this stage that the Congregation of the Propaganda Fidei in Rome concluded that a native clergy should be formed in each country so that Christians would not be left without priests in times of persecution, as had happened in Sri Lanka.

THE EUCHARIST IN DUTCH TIMES (1656–1796)

The Dutch period is the most glorious period of the Eucharist in Sri Lanka. The Catholics were persecuted by the Dutch. The Mass was forbidden. Severe fines and imprisonment were threatened against those who participated in the eucharistic ceremonies or harbored priests. During the early years after 1656 the Catholics had no priests at all. Until Father Joseph Vaz came from India in 1687 the Catholics persevered in the faith on their own. Their faith was maintained by their group life, organized on a tribal basis. There were local religious leaders, *Muppus* and *Annavis*, for seeing to the temporal affairs and religious instruction.

Father Joseph Vaz entered Ceylon in the dress of a poor laborer, wearing a coarse cloth from waist to knee after the manner of the coolies. He came in disguise with his servant John, as the Dutch would not permit any priests to come in legally. As he was an Indian, he could easily pass for a Sri Lankan. Often he went about like a beggar or coolie. He had to identify the Catholics in Jaffna where he began his work. Within two years he had come to know the Catholics and they became bold enough to celebrate the Eucharist openly. In 1689 they were organized to have public services at Christmas in eight different places. In three of them Joseph Vaz said Mass in the presence of thousands of people. The Dutch authorities decided to strike against the Catholics on this Christmas night.

The Dutch Major, Hendrick Adriaan van Rheede, assembled at the fort in great secrecy a band of armed men, and at a given signal on Christmas night he ordered them to march in separate detachments to the several churches or oratories in which the people of Jaffna were piously and devoutly assembled to celebrate the festival of the nativity of Our Lord.

With the Hollander troops there went also pagan lascarins, and at their head Baba Patem, a pagan Kanarese, who is now the chief man under the government of the commissary, for paganism and heresy thus join hands. All these infernal wolves surrounded the flock of Christ assembled to worship the Lamb of God in the cave of Bethlehem. They spared neither sex nor age but pounced upon them all, despoiled them of what they had, and what is most shameful to say, even stripped the women of their garments, a thing which they resented more than all other affronts. They were all taken prisoners and dragged to the fort with every indignity. Still greater were the insults to which they submitted the sacred images. Some they profaned on the spot, with their usual hatred and scorn; others they took with them to insult at leisure with shameful actions under the eyes of the commissary. The prisoners, it is said, were more than three hundred: of these the women were set free, but the men were kept in prison. As the news of this spread over the kingdom, the Christians of the more remote places had time to hide their sacred images, but on the following day they went in search of the Christians and put them in prison like the others.

Of those detained, all were fined for disobeying the plakkaats of the Company except eight persons, believed to be leaders. These were set apart for severe punishment. One of them, Don Pedro, was scourged so unmercifully that he died of the effects. The seven others were condemned to labour in chains at the repairing of a fort. Father Vaz himself escaped (R. Boudens, *The Catholic Church in Ceylon under Dutch Rule,* Rome, 1957, pp. 92–93).

This shows a type of situation different from that prevailing under Portuguese times. Here the Eucharist was celebrated somewhat as in the times of the early Christians in the Roman Empire. Joseph Vaz was alone as a priest for nine years. Then a few more priests came from India over the years. All the same, their number was very few, never more than thirty for the whole country. They had immense territories to cover. Thus Father Jacome Gonsalvez looked after the Colombo and Negombo areas from his residence in Kandy.

When a priest went to any area he announced himself to the Catholics. By night the faithful were gathered together. Confessions were heard and Mass was celebrated in hiding. Private houses were usually the places for the Mass. The people accepted the priests in this manner. Priests had no distinctive dress during this long period of persecution in the Dutch territories. There were no big churches, no schools, no hospitals, no elaborate organizations, no fast means of transport, no properties. The Eucharist was the single meeting point of prayer, worship, and instruction. The priests lived as it were underground. The Mass was an underground service, in the sense of being not public. The following extract from the *Life of Fr. Jacome Gonsalvez* by Father S. G. Perera indicates the type of life led by the Christians then:

In the year 1708 he [Gonsalvez] set out from Kandy on the first day of Lent on an apostolic tour in his new district, and was kept busy for three months without a break in the city of Colombo alone. All religious exercises in Colombo had to be done in secrecy and under cover of night, and the priest was not to venture out on the streets except in disguise, and never remain long in any part of the town; and the house in which service is held was not to be known to any, even to the Catholics, save those who were to be summoned thither on a given day. At nightfall the priest enters the house in disguise: a hall is arranged for service and dismantled before dawn; all Catholics in the vicinity receive notice in time to assemble there in the course of the night without attracting attention, when other citizens are abed. Then with closed doors and sentinels posted, the priest begins to hear confessions, administer baptism, if necessary, give instruction in one or other and often in two languages, after which he says Mass, preaches and before daybreak goes into hiding in another house known only to a few of the trustiest Catholics, where he is carefully guarded and gets ready to go over the same programme next day in another house, generally at some distance from the former. In some streets inhabited almost entirely by Catholics there is a chapel, without any outward appearance of being such, but appearing to be a storehouse or "godown," as they used to be called, to which the men come. In this way, whether in a chapel or in a private house, without remaining two successive days in the same locality, the priest had to labour without rest for days on end. There was not on this occasion a single night without confessions to hear and baptisms to give. In the course of these three months Father Gonsalvez baptized as many as 1,300 (De Nobili Press, Madura, 1942, pp. 25-26).

The Oratorian priests led by Joseph Vaz were responsible for the development of the Catholic literature in Sinhala and Tamil. Jacome Gonsalvez was foremost in this historic work. In spite of the severe handicaps of the time, they found the means to write books, copy them assiduously, and teach the Christians the faith. They composed prayers and hymns and gave the people further means of persevering in the faith. Due to the scarcity of priests, the celebration of the Eucharist was rare; perhaps a few times a year at most. Since there was a price on priests' heads, the celebration of the Mass was not a routine formality. It meant very much to the community. It gave them sustenance and cohesion in difficult times. The Oratorians began also the use of the Sinhala and Tamil prayers and readings during the Mass alongside the Latin. This was the *Pooja Dhyana*—a meditative reading and reflection on the sense of the Eucharist and on what was said in Latin. The Oratorians, being Indians, were able to bring the liturgy closer to the language and culture of the people. This close relationship continued for over a century. In British times it was the rise of a Catholic middle class educated in English in the colleges and convents that led to the downgrading of prayer in Sinhala and Tamil. The revival taking place today harks back to an eighteenth-century tradition—without, of course, the Latin which was obligatory then.

Father Joseph Vaz was a person of very great initiative and dedication. He faced all manner of danger from disease, loneliness, and above all Dutch persecution. He was a contestant of the Dutch laws against the practice of the Catholic faith. With his helper John he went the length and breadth of the land for nine years on foot and by cart in the search for Catholics.

The Apostle of Ceylon was a very holy person who was intensely active in his chosen task and innovative in his methods. For him lifestyle was subordinate to his mission. If it was necessary to be a beggar or a "coolie" to be with his flock, he became one. So did many later missionaries. At the same time he valued highly the intellectual apostolate. He combined corporate works of mercy with intellectual witness. He was at home in the king's palace or in the huts of the persecuted Christians.

The missionaries lived in poverty. A letter of Father Manuel de Miranda states:

We have here neither subsidies nor stipends of any kind from the Christians, for we give our service *gratis.* . . . We do everything at our own cost, without asking them for any payment. . . . How can people who are scarcely able to form an idea of things eternal be brought to desire and embrace the Catholic faith if its ministers have not a father's bowels of charity for the needs of children, and do not suffer with them in their afflictions helping and consoling them without the least expectation of any temporal return? If we ask these Christians for anything how can we refute and put to shame the vile falsehood of the proverbial saying among the heretics that the purgatory of the Catholics is the pocket of the priests? (S. G. Perera, S.J., ed., *The Oratorian Mission in Ceylon,* p. 103).

The Oratorians did not have a policy of training natives for the priesthood. While there were (minor?) seminaries in Mannar and in Colombo in Portuguese times, the Oratorians could not establish any such institutions in the Dutch-controlled areas where most of the Catholics lived.

The 140 years of perseverance under Dutch persecution made a significant difference to the Catholics of Sri Lanka. They have in their historical consciousness a sense of being able to withstand difficulties. It has also meant that they do not have churches, treasures, and property coming down for three or four centuries, as in Kerala and the Philippines. This experience should help us also to understand and appreciate the resilience and creativity of the people in both the villages and the towns. To think that Christians today cannot accept change or adapt themselves to new situations and needs shows a lack of historical memory. For during those fourteen decades they did experience a different lifestyle. The whole external framework of Portuguese Christianity collapsed. Its foreign props disappeared. Yet, by and large, the people retained the substance of the faith.

The study of, and reflection on, this period of church history must be given much more importance in the seminaries, in catechesis, and in the general life of the church. It is a pity that the Catholic community in Sri Lanka has so little awareness of its own past. We have to be grateful to scholars like Father S. G. Perera, S.J., Father Gnana Prakasar, O.M.I., Bishop Edmund Pieris, O.M.I., and Robrecht Boudens, O.M.I., for their contribution to the knowledge of this period of Sri Lankan church history. Liturgical renewal should include such an awakening of consciousness. The furthering of the cause of beatification of Father Joseph Vaz should be more closely associated with an awareness of the history of the people of that period.

THE EUCHARIST IN BRITISH TIMES (1796–1948)

In the last three decades of Dutch rule the Catholics had a measure of religious freedom. Their priests were recognized by the Dutch government provided they took an oath of loyalty to that regime. When Colombo fell into the hands of the British East India Company on February 16, 1796, the new rulers continued the tolerance practiced by the Dutch in the last days while being left with an anti-Catholic code.

The British, unlike the Dutch, were not so opposed to the Catholics in their colonies such as Ceylon (Sri Lanka). Their way of thinking was that the Catholics, too, as Christians, would be better allies of the British regime than believers of the other native religions. Hence they liberated the Catholics from the penal laws and gave full liberty to the Catholic church in Ceylon on May 27, 1806. The Catholics were thus emancipated in Ceylon a few decades prior to the Catholic emancipation in Britain itself in 1829. Catholics then numbered about 67,000.

The British, however, patronized the church of England, which became the established religion of the rulers. In the early British period social favor was for the followers of the Anglican church and other Protestant Christian groups. The Protestants had the advantage of an English education thanks to British and American missionaries, and hence those families which opted to be Protestant, particularly Anglican, advanced socially and economically sooner and faster than any of the others.

It was in this situation during the fourth and fifth decades of the nineteenth century that Catholics in Ceylon agitated for missionaries from Europe so that they too could have an English education. Rome also was concerned about the reorganization of the missions without dependence on the Portuguese Padroada with special rights of the Portuguese crown concerning missionary activity. The British were happy to receive Catholic missionaries from European countries, as these would be a help in building up Christian groups, which they considered more loyal than others.

Thus we find the arrival of new missionaries from Europe in the 1840s and subsequently. The Oratorians from Europe, Silvestrine-Benedictines, Oblates of Mary Immaculate, and Jesuits were the principal missionary groups of priests in Ceylon from that period till about the early 1950s. These missionaries found that they had to regroup and reorganize the Catholics, who were dispersed, not well instructed, and not organized. They were just emerging after 150 years of persecution when they had been more or less underground.

During the nineteenth century there was a gradual reorientation of the Catholic church toward becoming increasingly a well-established religious group. The liturgy of the Mass became more and more a formal ceremony, without the attendant risks of the previous century. As the number of European missionaries increased and as English education spread among upper-class Christians, the accent was once more on the more westernized practices. The Roman ritual was more easily observed. The life of Catholics also changed toward a greater conformism in the political and social setup. They were not serious contestants even for religious reasons.

The organization of parishes developed gradually due to the hard work of the missionaries from Europe. Once more churches and schools could be built. The Catholics were regrouped and reorganized into parishes. An ecclesiastical system of administration was established with parishes and dioceses. The hierarchy was set up in Ceylon in 1886. The native clergy was rapidly developed during the early decades of this century. Gradually local priests and religious were able to take over the work of the parishes, schools, and social services.

The nature of the eucharistic life of the established Catholic communities depends very much on the clergy of the day. We can see this in British times. Gradually a type of residential clergy evolved in Ceylon. During the British period a new type of priestly work was developed in which the accent was on the administration of the parishes, the building up of institutions, especially of education, and, after the 1930s, of lay apostolate organizations. The priest became more a resident clergyman whose life was spent mainly with the parishioners and organized around church feasts, novenas, religious instruction, and parish administration. Priestly life thus became fundamentally concerned with the maintenance operations of the religious community.

The Catholic priest in British times had a more honored place in society, though he was not so favored as his Protestant counterpart. Still, in a way he belonged to the racial stock and way of life of the ruling Europeans. He had more influence and acceptance, if not power, than the Catholic priests of Dutch times. He could move freely with the British rulers and officials and thus be of help to the Catholics. The priesthood therefore became once again more acceptable to the social power structure of the country. The Catholic priest became one of the principal agents for the spread of English education. His testimonials were valuable for securing employment. He was in no way doubted as to his political loyalties to the British Empire. The influence of the Catholic priest on the political liberation of the people of Ceylon was indirect and long term through education and social services and not in such a way as to be suspect of disloyalty by the ruling powers. The way of life of the priest, especially in more recent decades, became attuned to that of a resident pastor or teacher. The Catholic priesthood in Ceylon had thus come a long way from what it was in the time of Joseph Vaz and the Dutch persecution. He was in fact considered, in British times, as some sort of an ally of the social, political, and economic setup of the day.

The Ceylonese native clergy also grew up in this fashion. They adopted western ways of life like other leaders of society. The theology and the lifestyle of the priesthood was conditioned to fit in with the setup in Europe and westernization in the country. As the organization of the church became more established in Ceylon, the Catholic priest, especially the native priest, tended to become more and more the man of the organization who had a set way of life and whose function was largely a maintenance operation even within the social system. The increasing numbers of the clergy helped to make the work even more institutionalized and residential. The division of dioceses, entrusted to the different congregations and their subsequent rigid organization also contributed to the division of the church into independent territorial jurisdictions so that the priests of Ceylon today do not know each other. They have no common pastorate for the whole country and are much less together than in the time when there were fewer priests in Ceylon, as under the Dutch persecution of even about a hundred years ago.

In British times there was a cultural break in the tradition of the church. The accent changed from Sinhala and Tamil to English. This was so in the liturgy too, especially in the urban areas and church institutions such as colleges and convents. The rapid expansion of the religious congregations of sisters increased the institutionalization of the church. Hymns, prayers, and devotions were again brought from Europe to their houses. This time they came from France, Italy, Belgium, Holland, Ireland, and Britain rather than from Portugal and Spain.

The cultural change related to a socio-political transformation. The Catholic community became increasingly a part of the privileged group in Ceylon. There were many poor Catholics, but relatively Catholics had more opportunities for social advancement, thanks specially to the network of very good schools built by them. Economically too the church became more prosperous. Many of the local families that benefited from the economic development under the British were Christians. Proportionately there were more Christians among the planters, public servants, merchants, executives, and professionals. The centers of affluence were the urban areas, especially in the western coastal belt. Here Christians were in larger numbers.

All this meant that the Eucharist too took on a conservative tone. The Christian community was busy with self-improvement. But it did not recognize the deep-seated exploitation that was going on in the country under the British Raj. In a certain sense it profited by the colonial system. At least the elite prospered; its institutions developed and its influence spread. We have thus a situation in which the Eucharist was celebrated in the plantation areas of the hill country without the rape of the land by the British companies being contested. The system of quasi-slave labor of the indentured Indian worker was implicitly tolerated, for it was not challenged. The priest celebrated the Eucharist in the coolie lines for the laborers. The colonial planter could go to the parish church in the distance. The priest was friendly to both the planter and the laborers. This may be charity. It may have been the only feasible or known approach then. However, it was a compromise of the Eucharist with one of the worst forms of exploitation that the nineteenth and twentieth centuries have known. It goes without saying that there was no question of challenging the unfair terms of trade involved in the whole colonial economic system. Nor were the Christian communities significant groups in the movement for political independence.

We have to reflect on these situations to understand the level of irrelevance or, rather, the extent of compromise to which the Eucharist had been brought (unconsciously, perhaps, or unwittingly) in those times. One can conceive of the distance between the Eucharist and the suffering of the masses in the villages, plantations, and slums when we compare those conditions with life in the seminaries. The seminary is where the priests are trained for their task of leader of the eucharistic service and preacher of the word of God. The seminaries were cut off from the life of the people. The young students never went home for six or seven years. They remained in their segregated institutions. They would never leave their rooms except in the cassock which marked them as consecrated persons. This was an obligation as well as a privilege. The dress of the European clergy was reimposed with a holy vigor. The eucharistic devotion was a most important part of priestly formation, but it had little to do with the suffering of the oppressed.

The future priests prayed morning and evening for six

long years in that lordly splendor of the Papal Seminary at
Ampitiya or in Colombo. They were blissfully ignorant of
the cruel fate of the poor workers in the estates, or of the
villagers chased away from their lands for the benefit of
the British companies. The seminarians read the breviary
in Latin, sang hymns in plain chant, went for walks in
groups, and had innocent fun at recreation. They swore
fidelity to orthodox doctrine and loyalty to the church.
Their moral theology was from European textbooks of a
generation or two earlier. These all had little to do with the
tragedy that was being enacted around them in the world
outside their cloistered sanctuary. They were trained in
obedience to all constituted authority. Their study of history had very little of a critical approach, except where
church interests were concerned. They were generally innocent of sociology and social analysis. Marxism was
anathema and the class struggle seemed unchristian.

Thus during the nineteenth century and first half of this
century the Eucharist had little to do with human liberation in Ceylon. This reflected the position of the Christian
community. This in turn was related to what was advan-
tageous for the elite within this group—the clergy and the
affluent influential laity. It also coincided with the concepts prevalent in the metropolitan churches which held
the levers of control over church policy and theology. The
theology of this period was almost totally borrowed from
the textbooks and spiritual writings of Europeans and
North Americans. There was no theology flowing from a
reflection on the local situation. The writings of Archbishop Christopher Bonjean in favor of the vernacular and
of the rural people are a significant exception. Even scho-
larly historians of the church had no social analysis,
though they helped evoke a nationalist trend. It was in this
frame of mind that Ceylon approached political independence from the British in 1948.

In saying this we do not mean to overlook the personal
sincerity and the exceptional contribution of the foreign
missionaries, local clergy, religious, and laity of that

period. Yet in order to be faithful to our tasks today we have to reflect on the past as honestly as we can.

THE EUCHARIST SINCE INDEPENDENCE (1948–)

We have referred in different sections of this book to changes that have been recently effected in the Catholic liturgy, especially since the Vatican Council of 1962–65. These have included the language change from Latin and English to Sinhala and Tamil, the position of the altar, the time of the Mass, the readings, the simplification of the ceremonies of the Mass, the practical abolition of the eucharistic fast, and the elimination of the celebration of many feasts of saints. In certain places the music has changed to more popular songs and tunes. Concelebration is more common. All these, of course, have not necessarily meant a change in the significance of the Eucharist with reference to human liberation.

The content of sermons has changed insofar as the theology of the clergy has been updated. The National Seminary in Kandy, established in 1955, has had currents of theology that are more related to human problems of a collective nature than earlier. This seminary too has had its ups and downs. At a time it was feared by the hierarchy that some professors there were too radical. Then the hierarchy took over the seminary administration from the Oblates of Mary Immaculate. This was a setback to the theological relevance of the seminary. It is to be hoped that this is only temporary. The clash of opinions between some of the staff and students, on one side, and most of the hierarchy, on the other, at least showed that some new thinking was beginning to express itself in the seminary and in Sri Lanka in general.

During the 1960s thinking concerning the Eucharist underwent changes in many groups. Generally the changes have taken place imperceptibly in people's minds. The reduction in the frequency of auricular confession is now remarked as a significant fact. It came about without anyone advocating it, or making a fuss about it. It means that people's views of their relationship to God too has changed somewhat. They would seem to have more confidence in a direct personal relationship to God and his pardon. In any case, this has changed very much the use of the time of the priests. There is now no rush for confessions even before Easter or big feasts. People are getting accustomed to receiving Communion more often than in the past.

The National Synod held in 1968 and 1969, in its Declaration on Christian Worship, contains sections which signify the acceptance of the social significance of the Eucharist:

28. Finally Christ is really present in the community.... Communion at the altar means that one is ready for Communion with one's neighbour in all his needs and pursuits.

29. The more hidden the face of our neighbour through poverty, hunger, imprisonment, homelessness or unemployment, the greater the possibility of our awakening to the glory of God by relating ourselves savingly to him. Communion rightly understood will involve a real sharing of all that we have. Such sharing, even at the level of breaking ordinary bread for the poor, involves a certain breaking of our political and economic patterns which assure security to the privileged few.

30. If Christians really profess to come together to break bread, it means that they are willing to be broken in terms of their comfort and security so that other men may be bound to them and to God in their self-sacrificing love. And sharing perishable bread is but the initial affirmation of the Eucharistic celebration. The further implications on the social, political, economic and religious planes can be immense.

31. The Christian community in whom the saving God is really present must be qualified by the hunger and thirst for justice. In the present historical situation of shocking social inequalities and injustices, the worshipping community must strive to be present at the points of crisis, growth and liberation of society, so that they may be followers of the Master who laid down His life for the community.

However there has not been much follow-up on the decisions of the National Synod in any significant area. The

synod was like the high-water mark of the official en-
thusiasm in the church for the implementation of Vatican
II. Thereafter, in the early 1970s, a more conservative
stance prevailed among the leadership of the church.
The many social changes that have taken place in the
country since Independence, such as the change in language in 1956, the school takeover in 1961, and the policies
of socialization from 1970 to 1977, have radicalized somewhat the thinking of the Christians. The world trends of a
personalist nature in favor of individual freedom and responsibility are also affecting their lives. In Sri Lanka now
Christians as a whole are much less socially conservative
than thirty or even ten years ago. Yet this has not found
clear expression in the Eucharist except where the priests
themselves take an initiative. The National Liturgical
Commission is still very much concerned with rubrics,
ritual, and texts. It is still very much subject to the initiative from Rome; and this is not helpful for relating to
human problems in Sri Lanka.

We have referred earlier to initiatives among youth
groups toward greater communication and social relevance in the liturgy. A few houses of religious take the
initiative in this, provided the priest is not opposed to it.
But by and large the Eucharist remains very much what it
has been over the past century, especially in the large
parish assemblies on Sundays. There is little relevance to
actual problems, especially where effective social change
is concerned. The charismatic movement, which is gaining
popularity, helps to introduce a certain amount of flexibility in the liturgy. It encourages personal prayer and group
communication. It has not yet shown that it can motivate
toward social justice effectively. It is in this situation that
we refer to the dilemma of priests in the next chapter.

If the Eucharist is to help persons toward self-realization and meet the challenge of an unequal and unjust
society, the church needs a more enlightened and dynamic
leadership. Is it too much to expect that the National
Liturgical Commission will shake itself out of its lethargic

inactivity. It seems to sin more by omission than by commission. Bogged down with formalist juridical details, it misses the substance of the life of the spirit and of religious experience. Hence it fails to respond to more basic and urgent personal and societal needs. Every now and then there is some excitement about possible improvements, but little really happens. Vatican II came and went. The National Synod was convoked, met, and passed into history. Its impact was minimal. We hope that in the changed circumstances of today a real new leadership will be forthcoming. Or should the push come from the periphery, as has happened in most liturgical changes of the last three to four decades in the universal church? This may be an indication of the need for more creativity among base groups including priests, religious communities, and lay associations.

Chapter IX

The Eucharist
and the Dilemma of Priests

The lifestyle of the clergy has a relation to the way the Eucharist is celebrated. At a time when kings lived in palaces, their Eucharistic celebrators also lived in palatial mansions. In some countries, to this day, the residences of bishops are called "palaces." But in recent decades some bishops have begun to live in ordinary rented apartments. More and more priests and religious are adopting simpler lifestyles. They are moving away from the solidly built rectories of parishes, for in these they are immunized against the sufferings of the mass of the people. As the clergy grow in these experiences, they begin to become aware of the real disunity and lack of communion covered by the blank homogeneity of the Sunday Mass in the average parish. The more sensitive among them become uneasy about their own participation in such a travesty of the true meaning of the Gospel of Jesus Christ.

I know of a city parish priest who questioned the meaning of a New Year dawn Mass when the revelers from a large hotel were straggling in for a quick Eucharist. They had ushered in the New Year at a 140-rupees-"per-soul" dance. Each couple had spent over 500 rupees for the night. For the same Mass the poorer city folk come in without a feast. They do not have 500 rupees for the whole family for two months. The still poorer do not come to this church, as it is too elite for them. Numerous beggars stand at the church doors and line themselves at the gate. After Mass the very rich give a few coins to these beggars. Thus the human caravan continues Sunday after Sunday, week after week, year after year, decade after decade, and in fact century after century. Where then is the "common union" of the Eucharist?

SELF-QUESTIONING BY PRIESTS

One of the reasons for the recent exodus from the priesthood is the irrelevance and even positive harmfulness of the way in which the Eucharist is celebrated. The Mass and the care of the Eucharist are among the priest's principal functions. When he begins to lose faith in its actual impact he begins to question the meaning of his whole life. He sees how much he is part of a system that he can hardly change. He feels he is used to justify an unjust power distribution. He may bring personal consolation to individuals but hardly sees himself as related to overall societal changes. These latter are considered necessary for effective love in a community. He then begins to question even his concept of love. Is it enough merely to be loving without wanting to change unjust situations? Can he merely serve progressives and conservatives in juxtaposition at the eucharistic table without wanting to change them to effective action? Is the Eucharist neutral to justice?

On the other hand, if the priest becomes involved in social issues he finds he has to take options on day-to-day problems. He sees that some of his parishioners exploit others. Some in fact take the food away from others who are hungry. Some have much land, others none. Some spend much on private transport, health, and education, while others have broken-down, overcrowded, ill-staffed public buses, hospitals, and schools. Some are black-marketeers. Some even torture others. As the priest perceives these incongruities his conscience becomes troubled. He asks himself if he is doing the right thing. Is he making the best use of his consecrated life? Can he afford to tell these things in his sermons? Will he be supported by his superiors if he does so? What will the "faithful" say?

Will he be "reported" to the bishop as a troublemonger, an unbalanced person, one involved in politics, a "Communist"? What will the bishop then think, say, and do? How will his friends, fellow priests, relatives, and parents react to such a social sensitivity? After all, many fellow priests who thought like him and tried to react conscientiously are now in exile, or have left the priesthood. Many are married. He may even begin to doubt his vocation.

It is necessary that there be a more general understanding of the trauma of the contemporary priest. This is particularly true of the young and middle-aged priests. The older priests may be so ingrained in their views and relationships that they do not experience these doubts. Those who are younger may see them and seek another vocation in the lay state while they are still young enough. Many former priests are now married. But it would be incorrect to think that it is always the desire for marriage that makes them discontented with the priestly life. Very often this is not so. On the contrary, it is often the sense of irrelevance, futility, and the lack of an identity in their priestly lives that lead them to move away from this vocation. The general absence of dynamic leadership within the official church adds to their discomfiture.

Today the number of clergy is decreasing. This is quite apparent in northern Europe, where the trend began nearly three decades ago. In English-speaking countries like the United States, Britain, Canada, Australia, New Zealand, and even Ireland the number of clergy is falling. Many religious congregations are selling their large scholasticates in Rome and elsewhere, as these have become large empty shells with few aspirants to the priesthood.

In Sri Lanka the problem of vocations is being felt acutely. The Archbishop of Colombo in a statement in May 1977 mentioned the shortage of priests as a principal problem. In the Colombo Archdiocese one priest has to manage parishes of 10,000 to 12,000 believers, where there had been two or three priests earlier. In institutions with ten priests formerly, now there are only three or four. The average age of the clergy is rising. There are many on the quasi-retired list, doing some marginal service, such as being chaplain to an orphanage or home for the aged. Above all, the expectation of younger reinforcements is decreasing. For twenty-five years we have not received foreign missionaries. The forecast for new priests for Colombo from the local seminary is bleak, at least for the next few years.

In my experience as chaplain of the International Movement of Catholic Students in Asia and in conferences for clergy, religious, and bishops, I have seen how deep-rooted this problem is in the different Asian countries. Everywhere the priests are beginning to question the meaning of their ministry. The Eucharist is, naturally, central to this preoccupation. Some among the more dedicated and dynamic are very active in the struggles for human rights and social justice. A few have been or are in prison. Some foreign missionaries have been repatriated, due to their involvement in action for human liberation. A few have evolved new lifestyles in relation to workers and peasants in the villages, factories, and slums. The bulk of the clergy, however, remain as before, doing their traditional work. But as awareness of social issues dawns on them, they begin to sense the inadequacy, incompetence, and even counterproductivity.

The youth, including students, are conscious of these problems. They sense the dilemma of their chaplains, priest-teachers, and administrators. They are not generally impressed by the social conservatism of the Eucharist, even if they themselves are not progressive. The decline in the priestly vocations from among the university students is remarkable. This is in notable contrast to the position in countries like India and Sri Lanka some decades ago. The alienation of youth from the priesthood has a relationship to their not finding meaning in the large-scale parish Masses and services given by the clergy.

When rumblings among the clergy began to be heard the first reaction of those in authority was to stress the hard line of conformity to the prevailing norms of the church. Little effort was made in Sri Lanka to understand the deep nature of the disaffection among the priests with their own state of life. The lay people, too, were rather hard in their criticism of any desire for change. Many worthy priests were sent into exile due to this combination of circumstances. During the past fifteen years at least sixty priests of Sri Lanka have left the priesthood, gone to Europe or America, or opted for some other type of ministry without direct responsibility for the work of the official church. This is about one-tenth of the country's clergy. This is a large number compared to the position from 1930 to 1955 or so when hardly any priest left the priesthood or defected from the line given by the official authority in the dioceses. Such a phenomenon cannot be blamed merely on the individual priests. It has to be taken in conjunction with the considerable exodus from the ranks of the religious brothers and sisters—perhaps over one hundred of them—and the steady decline in the number of priestly ordinations. Even among priests who still continue the regular parish ministry or work in private schools, there is a radical questioning of the meaningfulness of their work. Such questioning is now being heard in the ranks of the episcopacy also.

The issues are much wider than the eucharistic celebration as such. They touch the whole life of the church, and the very idea of religion itself. Yet since the Eucharist is central to the Christian community, as well as the life of the priest, the problems within the ranks of the priesthood reveal also a malaise concerning the eucharistic practice in the church. Both the church leaders and the Christian people at large must reflect seriously on this. For no community can live a healthy life when its full-time servants, ministers, and officials suffer such an identity crisis and lack of a sense of meaning. Perhaps this crisis is not limited to Christianity only. It may have a wider significance in the whole process of secularization in our day. It is important that Christians understand these issues. With more sensitivity to what the others are thinking and feeling, much heartbreak can be avoided. I am aware of the deep suffering of many mothers and fathers at the way their priest-sons have been treated by Christians, including responsible authorities. Sometimes this suffering is further aggravated by the lack of understanding between parents and children, or even between the two parents themselves. The Roman authorities and liturgical commissions must take these issues seriously. It is not enough to insist on ancient rules or new norms. An effort must be made to understand the mind and heart of the people and priests of this generation. They should not think that a lack of conformity to rigid liturgical norms is necessarily due to an absence of a spiritual sense, or of seriousness in life. On the contrary, the new consciousness of spiritual life itself is making some priests and others rethink their whole life, including the forms of worship and prayer. The older priests must be willing to listen to the younger ones and learn to accept them even when they may not be disposed fully to understanding them. The young ones must be careful not to shock the older ones beyond what they can cope with. Yet some clash is inevitable and not necessarily bad. If those in authority and seniority do not understand the mood, the trend, and the aspirations of the more radical youth, the result will be disastrous for the church as it is at present constituted.

Neither should it be thought that the demand for radical changes in the liturgy comes from a lessening of devotion to Jesus Christ. Rather, it is due to a deeper understanding of the nature of the priesthood of Jesus as the one and only high priest of the New Testament. A closer relationship is seen between Jesus as priest and victim, between the Eucharist and the cross, and between his death and his action for human liberation. The better inspirations in the contemporary priesthood are in this direction. In fact it is a loyalty to Jesus Christ that brings to many an inner compulsion to question radically the rigidity and social conformism of the prevailing liturgical practices and norms.

One can however counsel serious openness to these issues. We can have confidence that the concern for the spiritual values will continue in the coming years and decades; but the present forms of liturgy and priesthood are in grave danger of obsolescence if there is no radical reorientation in their values and approaches.

THE CLASH OF INSTITUTION AND CONSCIENCE

The crisis concerning the Eucharist brings into relief quite clearly the deeper dilemma in the minds of many priests. It is a clash of loyalties, of the claims of the organized institution as against those of the priest's persistent inner conscience. One demands conformity; the other counsels authenticity. He sees that what the church law prescribes largely alienates his people from real virtue; but what his conscience urges can hardly be reconciled with the prevailing law and practice concerning the Eucharist. The changes promulgated by church authorities are generally too piecemeal, rather half-hearted, and usually too late.

On the other hand, the priest knows that his people want a religious expression of their faith. They want a liturgy, a public worship, a common prayer, and even a colorful celebration. The people's desires depend on the "faith" they have imbibed. Then faith depends on the beliefs taught by the priests and the traditions of the community. The more searching priest knows that this "simple faith" is to a good extent determined by the very social conditioning of the church over the centuries. He discerns a gap between such a faith and a more enlightened acceptance of the fundamental teachings and values of Jesus of Nazareth. Hence he feels uneasy about his own work, his continuance of this type of belief and worship.

Yet he cannot so easily change things. The people as a whole are also liturgically conservative. Or rather, the conservatives dominate the church's public worship. The more radical keep away. So do the more lax. The priest therefore wants to retain the loyalty of the 40 or 50 percent of the Catholics who frequent the Eucharist. Hence he must not shock them too much. He must not disturb their tranquillity in the concept of faith they hold. Thus the pressure of the law, of the authority, and of those who come to the services is toward a basic liturgical conservatism. This is true in spite of gradual external changes over the past fifteen years.

If, however, the priest wishes to relate the Eucharist to real issues in his areas, he is involved in further problems. His whole training in the seminary and as a priest has been to exercise leadership in the traditional sacral fashion. The priest has been taught to expect the respect of the people. The people still reverence the priest for his role, especially in the liturgy. Many priests are not quite capable of other roles in personal relations or social groups. They do not get the same reverence outside the liturgical framework. In the liturgy they exercise a privileged position. They claim the power to preside over the Eucharist, to make Jesus present on the altar. They exercise a monopoly in this sphere. The people are dependent on them for divine sustenance. Hence they naturally prefer to emphasize the importance of the *ex opere operato*—by their very conferring—effect of the Eucharist; that is, its impact depends on the action of the celebrant rather than on his dispositions or those of the people, namely, *ex opere operantis.*

Were the priest to engage in a process of enlightening the people on the deeper meaning of the Eucharist as a call to effective sharing, there is a likelihood that the whole life of the priest, and of the community, would begin to be questioned. He would lose the automatic self-importance given by the prevailing eucharistic law. But he seldom has other ways of giving himself or of feeling so wanted. Hence the built-in pressure within him to conserve the liturgical status quo with minor changes. The bishops feel this pressure even more, for the bishops claim the monopoly of ordaining priests and fellow bishops. Their dominion over the faithful is through their control over the clergy. This latter is maintained by the power given to priests for performing the liturgical rites. Hence this very authority depends in the present dispensation on the hold they have over the institution, not to mention the financial dependence of their clergy on the diocesan authorities. Even finances are related to the Mass as a source of income-generation. Thus the whole life of the institution is closely related to eucharistic practices. We say this not to de-emphasize the Eucharist, but to try to see how, actually, eucharistic life is organized today.

With the people being more aware and more socially conscious there is likely to be a greater demand for a more meaningful Eucharist. As the theology of the seminaries and of the younger clergy evolves in a more socially committed direction, these clergy will feel urged toward more fundamental changes in the liturgy. If the country also moves in a more socialist direction with freedom, then there would be external pressure on the churches to change; and this too would be felt in the eucharistic celebration. It is, however, noteworthy that in socialist countries which are dictatorial, little freedom is left for the churches to innovate in the liturgy. Even the content of the sermons is controlled. The Eucharist in such circumstances is a space of free meeting which the governments jealously watch. The priests in such conditions tend to be socially tame. If not, they will find it difficult to continue as leaders in public worship.

Over the years the Eucharist will be an index of the social and personal relevance of the church. The priests will be deeply involved in this. The future of the priesthood as it is at present will be largely dependent on how the Eucharist will relate to integral human liberation following the example of Jesus himself. Unless a fair proportion of the priests share and experience the oppression and suffering of the poor, the priesthood as such will not know what it is to be exploited and underprivileged. Until they participate in the struggles of the masses they will not understand the exigencies of the cause of human liberation. But if these trends take shape and grow, then, one hopes, the priesthood itself will be reinvigorated. Fortunately this is already taking place in a small measure in many countries, especially in North and South America.

THE DILEMMA OF THE CHURCH

In the context of the decreasing numbers of priests and their increasing age, the churches are faced with a new problem. Up to recent times the clergy formed a socially respected profession. There was always a demand to enter its ranks. Today with secularization this is less so. The clergy who exercise a role of influence in the building of a new type of society are still few. In the socialist countries of Eastern Europe they are respected as being closer to the people and not belonging to the dominant Communist party. Even the antireligious propaganda has not succeeded in destroying the respect for them; it may even give some influence to them indirectly.

The problem is further complicated for the Catholic church due to its insistence on clerical celibacy. Here there are two problems: the relevance of the priesthood and the obligation of celibacy. The Catholic church in West European countries is now facing the problem of a shortage of priests. Many parishes have no priests. As the priests grow older, their dynamism and initiative decrease. This is remarked in religious orders and congregations too. It is now a rather rare sight to see a young sister, brother, or priest in a country like France.

One consequence of this is that some functions of the priest are taken over by the laity. The question then arises as to what are the functions which lay persons cannot perform. Another trend is the grouping of parishes under a few priests who ensure the essential services with quicker means of communication. But these actions do not resolve the problem. The ordination of married persons and optional marriage for the clergy are no longer alternatives that are totally excluded from consideration. The ordination of women has been accepted by certain Protestant churches. Whatever its decision the Catholic church is faced with a serious problem concerning its own way of life.

THE END OF THE CLERICAL CHURCH?

The Catholic church has depended for centuries on its ordained clergy for its work of evangelization, administration, and worship. There was an abundance of full-time celibate, male clergy. They were freed from the burden of earning a living outside church institutions. People came to them for their ministrations and they felt wanted and fulfilled as persons. Today, after Vatican II, the situation has changed substantially in Western Europe. Celibacy and male priesthood remain the norm. The church authorities have refused to accept any changes. But many priests now work in secular employment. In France about 750 priests are today thus employed. They are worker-priests, if not priest-workers. They earn their living by work. Hence they are less dependent on the ecclesiastical structures for their sustenance or even moral acceptance for liturgical functions. They live closer to the people and share more their life conditions.

This is an evolution in the form of the priesthood which is quite marked now, even though Vatican Council II could not foresee it. It implies a somewhat different attitude toward the one who presides at the Eucharist or preaches. He is no longer fully cut off from lay life. Perhaps this indicates one way in which this problem may be faced. Or is it only a particular solution for this generation of priests. Will future youth enter seminaries to be ordained for such a work?

A significant long-term question for African and Asian countries is that there will not be so many full-time celibate clergy to run the church administration from Western Europe. For some time Africans and Asians will be imported and incorporated into the offices of the Vatican and the religious congregations. But it is difficult to see how after a decade or fifteen years Western European clerics will be able to continue their traditional role of ruling the church. This will mean a new situation for churches in Asia, Africa, and Latin America. Already Africans and Asians are in important positions in Rome. Yet they are few and of a generation that can be made to accept "Romanità," the Roman way, and even ecclesiastical career service. But as the numbers of these increase something similar to what happened at the United Nations may take place in the Catholic church too. The peoples from the periphery may outnumber the main western powers. At this stage a question would be whether it is better to declericalize the administration in order to keep it white and western or Afro-Asianize it to preserve its clerical position. This too is no long-term solution. For even in Asian countries there is a reduction in the numbers of the clergy. It is said that in terms of quality the standards are lower now than in the past.

Many in the church turn a blind eye to the oncoming crisis of the Catholic priesthood. Yet it is a most significant one and will change the external presentation of the church. It will also raise deeper issues concerning the nature of ministry in the church. This in turn will lead to questions regarding lifestyle, ministry, ecumenism, tradition and innovation, the example of Jesus Christ, and the very nature of the church. The Christian communities are set on a course of change which will gather in depth and rapidity with each succeeding year and decade. We would do well to be aware of them to be able to retain the basics of the Gospel of Jesus Christ while meeting these changes.

Chapter X

Renewal of the Eucharist and Human Aspirations

Whether we look to the Old Testament, the example of Christ, or the needs of society today, the Eucharist has to be related positively to human liberation if it is to be faithful to its origins and its performance. It has to lead Christian communities to analyze the issues which confront persons and the human community today, to an unmasking of injustices, and to building groups for liberation. Already, in many countries, the Eucharist is taking on this meaning. In this sense Christians are once again undertaking, in certain places, the long march for the reform of themselves and their societies; and the Eucharist is the manna during their march in the desert.

If there is to be truthfulness in the celebration, the Eucharist should deepen faith and commitment. It should tend toward effective building of unity, first among those who participate in the Eucharist, and thereby the rest of society. For God is with us only when there is a genuine growth of *love* among human beings. For us union with God is possible only through service to others and in building human unity. The teaching of Jesus concerning the parable of the Good Samaritan shows us the importance of effective action in society toward our neighbor. Today almost everywhere in the world people face grave difficulties due to shortages of essential commodities, including food. This is often brought about by exploitation of the many by the powerful rich.

SOME CURRENT TRENDS

Today, fortunately, we see a return to the deeper meaning of the Eucharist, at least among some groups. The emphasis is not on the number of Masses, nor on the obligation of weekly Mass, but rather on the depth of commitment of oneself and the group to the values of Christ in the world around. There is much more flexibility in participation. The sermon is not a monologue by the priest celebrant; instead the homily is shared. It is related to events affecting the participants and the wider society. There is much more spontaneity. The rigid distances of the big churches are replaced by the closeness of persons who communicate with each other seriously. The repentance of sins is more collective. The Communion of the Body of Christ is preceded by an effort at human communion among the participants. Building community outside is sought through action, thought out together in Communion. We are thus returning to a type of Eucharist of which the Acts of the Apostles speaks.

The communication process leads to transformation within families, in groups, and in bigger communities such as parishes. Such celebrations are particularly meaningful for groups engaged in movements for personal and social change. Naturally it has to begin with small groups that are prepared to communicate with each other honestly. The experiences of modern group formation, of charismatic renewal, and community renewal find expression in a liturgy that has been reinvigorated by this flow of life coming mainly from action groups engaged in a struggle or from committed contemplatives, rather than from the official custodians of the rite. This evolution may still seem unofficial, and even suspect to many of the more orthodox minds; but these are the trends of a new life that is leading to a rediscovery of the more vital meaning of the Eucharist.

The Eucharist, believed in seriously, is challenging the lifestyle of the more affluent. They begin to feel uneasy

with the way they live. They question the policy orientations of the countries in which they live, and of the groups
to which they belong. Sometimes this leads to changes in
lifestyles, to pooling of resources, to greater sharing, to
involvement in action for justice. But these changes do not
take place suddenly or in big crowds. It is due to a sustained reflection and communication in depth of the better
inspirations of persons in a group that such a degree of
sharing takes place.

Sometimes the Eucharist leads to integration of persons
in commitment; at other times the involvement in issues
leads persons to seek meaning in shared prayer and in
eucharistic communion. The choice of texts, music, songs,
prayers depends very much on the group, its preoccupations, and its level of involvement and communication.
Fortunately, the texts now prescribed by the official
liturgy lend themselves more to such commitment. In
some countries many new songs have been composed and
have become popular in the last decade. They are more
concerned with values such as love, sharing, friendship,
justice, truth, peace, freedom, liberation, struggle, suffering, joy, resurrection.

The Eucharist is also organized by different groups according to their interests: for example, workers, youth,
students, religious, families. There is more spontaneity
and room for different cultural expressions than in the
past. The peace movement in the United States, the liberation theology in Latin America, and the action groups in
Europe have been concerned with a more relevant worship. In Africa and Asia there is a growth of indigenous
religious music. The Indian Rite Mass that has been accepted by the Catholic bishops of India incorporates many
aspects of Indian culture within the Eucharist.

While appreciating these trends we think that a much
greater transformation is required if the liturgy is to try to
respond to the needs of persons and the world today. The
church is only slowly coming up from the rear, while the
world rushes ahead in its overall development.

A DEEPER ORIENTATION IS REQUIRED

Our reflection on the Eucharist shows that the problem of giving meaning to it is not merely one of minor changes of an external nature such as in the form of celebration, types of songs, language, and ritual. It is only as a community becomes more committed to each other and society that its eucharistic celebration will become more meaningful. Hence, our preoccupation has not to be so much with the eucharistic service for its own sake but, rather, with the building of a real sharing community that is concerned with the whole society. Hence, the eucharistic community has to be a conscious, reflective, action-oriented group and not just a haphazard collection of individuals who come together merely for the ceremonial observance. A meaningful Eucharist, therefore, requires freedom, spontaneity, interpersonal communication, authenticity, and a genuine relationship of love and justice toward a wider environment.

This also means that a parish of one thousand or five thousand or ten thousand persons cannot easily become a relevant group for a meaningful and truthful eucharistic celebration. A parish is more an administrative division and it is useful for the purposes of maintaining ecclesiastical unity, but it is not necessarily the community of persons who seek together to give their lives for the values of the kingdom. If such big parishes are to exist as groups for eucharistic celebration, they must find the means for effective self-examination, societal analysis, communication, and action. As yet, we are far from such an approach.

A reflection on the Eucharist also raises the question of the nature of the priesthood and the need of the ordained minister for presiding at the eucharistic celebration. Here, too, the primary value is not the rank or the person insofar as she or he is given status and power by ordination but the degree and nature of his or her involvement to build love and justice in community and his or her acceptance as such by the eucharistic community itself. As a renewal in the

Eucharist takes place, there has to be also a deep rethinking and change in the idea of the priesthood, the lifestyle of the priest, and in his or her self-giving in the cause of integral human liberation.

He or she would then become more and more the true animator of a real community of love and sharing, and cease to be the mere functional president of a controlled ritual. The churches, too, as institutions must have the insight and the courage to meet this challenge.

The institution of the Eucharist also reveals the genius of Jesus as a spiritual leader. He transformed the elaborate Jewish liberation ceremonial into a simple, meaningful community reunion that had revolutionary potentialities of transforming persons and communities. The Acts of the Apostles bears witness to this.

The Eucharist has an extraordinary potential for being an agent of personal and global transformation. Every week about 200 million persons meet all over the world in Christian communities. The Sunday celebration is perhaps the most numerous regular gathering of human beings around a common theme that this world knows. If it is vitalized into being truly a sacrament of communion through effective sharing, it can be the most efficacious means of bringing about the radical cultural revolution required among Christians. And if Christians practice what the Lord has taught, many of the world's problems would be solved both at a structural and personal level.

The renewal of the Eucharist can come about only with a growth of the commitment of believers to the fundamental message of Christ. This is in turn possible only through a process of death to consumerism, to the seeking of power and prestige, and to organized selfishness. The Eucharist will thus be a continuing process of purification of persons and institutions—hopefully leading us closer to the promised land and more fulfilling interpersonal relations within the limits of our human potentialities.

In the light of what has been said earlier the liturgy

today has to face further challenges beyond its present evolution since Vatican II. Whereas the liturgy of earlier centuries was geared toward personal salvation in an individualistic sense, the building of the church and thereby the glorifying of God, we have now to relate to new needs, such as:

(i) personal fulfillment with freedom and responsibility
(ii) the realization of the values of justice, truth, freedom, love, equality, and peace within human societies
(iii) the building of a just world order and a new humanity
(iv) communion with cultures, religions, and ideologies that are not of Christian inspiration
(v) the growth of the Christian communion in the service of the human person and the world

These require a deep personal and interpersonal reflection, new theological accents, socio-political analysis and options, action and evaluation, forming of alliances, risk-bearing, new lifestyles, new modes of being a Christian community, a spirituality of the person and of the human community, and so forth. How can the liturgy contribute to these different dimensions of human spiritual need?

The push of the world toward such meaningfulness can be welcomed by the church as a sign of the action of God teaching us through the quest of persons for more union with the Absolute within the daily realities of life. The world has entered the sanctuary and wishes to relate it to the concern of the people of the world.

We suggest two main trends in this further development of Christian worship, (1) with reference to the aspirations of men and women of our time, and (2) specifically in relation to the cultures and religions of Asia. The two are also interrelated because Asia is being modernized and because there is in the western world a greater search for spiritual meaning in the Asian religious traditions and practices, such as Zen and Yoga. Today these traditions belong to the patrimony of humanity.

THE ANTHROPOLOGICAL DIMENSION
IN WORSHIP

The renewal of contemporary theology has been greatly due to this concern and to that connected with a deeper understanding of the word of God. It was one of the leitmotifs of Vatican Council II, running through most of its discussions and decisions. The Constitution on the Church in the Modern World expresses it beautifully and powerfully:

The joys and the hopes, the griefs and the anxieties of the men of this age, especially those who are poor or in any way afflicted, these are the joys and hopes, the griefs and anxieties of the followers of Christ. Indeed, nothing genuinely human fails to raise an echo in their hearts. For theirs is a community composed of men. United in Christ, they are led by the Holy Spirit in their journey to the Kingdom of their Father and they have welcomed the news of salvation which is meant for every man. That is why this community realizes that it is truly linked with mankind and its history by the deepest of bonds (no. 1).

As we have already seen, the Old Testament tradition of the psalms and the celebration of the great deeds of God had an intimate connection with the history and struggles of the Jewish people. The Exodus was a liberation from slavery and a pledge of the promised land flowing with milk and honey. The story of creation was a guarantee of God's undying concern for his children. The events of history, including success and failure, victory and defeat, carried with them the enlightening word of God to his chosen people.

The New Testament purified the concept of the kingdom of God from being too material; yet it did not remove it from a deep link with humankind and its history. The incarnation, the paschal mystery, and the new pentecostal times involved the whole human race. They bore the central message of God's deliverance for all. The apostles understood the deep connection between liturgy and life, as is witnessed by the Acts of the Apostles. For they gave themselves to prayer and the breaking of bread; they held all things in common and there was no one in need among them. There was a direct link between worship and service, between prayer and witness to love. Christ and the Old Testament prophets continually referred to the vital necessity of this bond, which is also the gauge of the sincerity of religious rites and of sacrifices. Its absence was one of the main pillars of Pharisaism, for they prayed with their lips to be seen by men; but their hearts were hard and unsympathetic to human suffering and even exploitation.

The natural seasons, the needs and festivities of the agricultural communities, and the rites and celebrations of the then prevailing religions had a significant influence on the development of the Christian liturgy, including the Roman rites. Ancient feasts and rites were "baptized"; the Christian mysteries were, as it were, superimposed on them. The rogation days, the litanies, and even feasts such as Christmas bear witness to this process.

As the liturgy became organized and structured and as the central authority of the Latin church grew stronger, there was little opportunity for further adaptation. Saints were added to the calendar. These naturally reflected the rather monastic concepts of sanctity; popes, bishops, priests, monks, virgins, and widows were the main types of persons canonized. Few laypersons who lived an ordinary lay life in the world were thought of as saints.

New Themes

We are today in a world different from medieval feudal society; hence radical changes, especially in content, are required for relevance to the hopes and joys, the griefs and anxieties of the men and women of this age.

A consideration of these interests suggests certain themes that must form part of the modern Christian's instruction, reflection, mission, and witness. These themes should therefore find a place in the liturgy in some form.

They should form a point of departure for Christian reflection and a point of return for dedicated action. The liturgy—along with catechesis—can mediate between reflection and action. The liturgy and catechesis would then help give an orientation to the action of the Christian community at all levels.

The liturgy should be reorganized to provide for personal and collective reflection on themes such as:

Food: eating, fasting, famine;

Clothing: needs, cold, uses, fashions;

Shelter: needs, slums and shanties, inequalities, remedies;

Family: parents' days, father's day, mother's day, women, children, youth, teenagers, the aged, the child, divorce, abortion, family planning;

Sex and Marriage: family life, women's rights;

Environment: pollution, waste, care of nature;

Health: disease, medicine, social services, doctors, nurses, world health (Good Samaritan);

Education: ignorance, needs, schools, universities, mass media, radio, TV, newspapers, books (Press Sunday);

Work: employment, unemployment, wages, conditions of work;

Leisure: availability, use, orientation, cinema, sports, music, arts;

Freedom: human personality development, independence day, love and service, church of service, disinterested charity;

Transport: needs (public, private), accidents, tourism;

Public Life: government, political parties, companies, corporations;

Truth: honesty and sincerity in public and private life, respect for truth from whatever source it comes;

Justice: social justice within the nation, capitalism, socialism, racial harmony, human rights;

Religious Harmony: wider ecumenism, tolerance, cooperation among religions, Christian unity, ecumenism (Unity Week), mission of the church;

Groups: workers' day (May 1st), farmers, industrialists, teachers, Pope's day, bishops, thanksgiving day;
World Justice: United Nations, UNCTAD, seas, action groups.

New Themes and the Christian Mystery

These themes must be understood as intimately connected with the mystery of Jesus Christ and the mission of the church in the world. They should not distract our minds in any way from the core of the Christian message and reality, but rather give deeper meaning and significance to it and incarnate it in the very heart of the lives of people of our age. They will enable people to participate more intelligently, more actively, and more meaningfully in the liturgy.

Naturally such themes are more exacting in terms of Christian witness: hence they are well suited to make the sacramental life more closely connected with life and more realistic. At present there is too much of a belief in the mere *ex opere operato* aspect of the sacraments. This is partly responsible for dulling the Christians' consciousness of their social and civic responsibilities. It may also partly explain why others seem to suspect that Christians think they have found a rather facile way to salvation through the sacramental life. But the sacraments should normally lead us to a deeper commitment to the duties of the position in life that they signify.

Meditation on these themes could help to render the witness of the church more relevant to humankind and hence the church would be a better sign of Jesus Christ's love for all people. Christians would thus be helped to move out of any ghettos into which they might have receded in certain areas. The life of priests and religious would also find more meaning in such an orientation of the liturgy. The liturgy could thus help to maintain the necessary dualism and tensions between the word of God and the demands of the human situation; it could be purified of its irrelevant sentimentality and taken right into the midst of the struggle between good and evil that is constantly being waged within every person and society.

These themes are not only the expression of some of our fundamental problems and aspirations today; they are also in keeping with a renewed theology that better sees the role of terrestrial reality in God's plan. They are closer to the moral values presented in the Sermon on the Mount, which is so appealing to all people of goodwill. The Sermon on the Mount presents a morality that is at the same time God-centered and human-oriented. The teaching of Christ in St. Matthew about the criteria of the final judgment relates likewise to our relationships to our neighbor as the measure of our orientation to God. Hence a concern with the deep values involved in the human situations and struggles of today is at the same time a concern with God's plan of salvation. God takes human beings seriously—as his whole plan of redemptive love indicates. It is therefore necessary that in the worship of God we too take human beings seriously. This is not a detraction from the honor due to God but, rather, a greater attentiveness to him.

In such a renewal of themes we should also reconsider the accent to be placed on different aspects of the Christian mystery. Thus, in the liturgy a better utilization of the significance of *Creation* for human relations with God and among human beings themselves would be very desirable. Our concepts of human rights, racial harmony, social justice, development, and work are all fundamentally based on the fatherhood of God and the task assigned to humankind on earth. The present texts of the liturgy may have many references to Genesis, but they should be so presented as to make their relevance to modern issues more clear and inspiring.

Similarly the final *orientation of the world to God* should be better brought out through the eschatological references. At present those invoked are rather negative, speaking of destruction and judgment. They could be counterbalanced with others referring also to the role of people in building the new heaven and the new earth. This should help to motivate the human commitment to the development of the world, to world peace and harmony. The liturgy had of old also the function of *instructing catechumens*, as is seen from the readings in the period of Lent. At present many missionaries in Asia ask now to instruct catechumens in such a way that they are brought from their normal human preoccupations to an understanding of the Christian mystery. A restructuring of the liturgy with more explicit inclusions of some of these themes would greatly help the catechumens who might then participate more profitably in the service of the Word either prior to the Eucharist or otherwise.

The *Liturgical Year* could be conceived of in such a way as to correspond to some extent to the human calendar of countries today with their different celebrations, for example, United Nations Day, Children's Day, World Peace or War Memorial days, Independence days, Thanksgiving Day, May Day, and the like. The church could also initiate celebrations which might eventually lead to a universal reflection on some of these values and problems. There could also be an arrangement of the calendar of saints and patron saints in a manner that would be more appropriate to our times. It is, of course, understood that the main liturgical cycle would be preserved while these themes are introduced more explicitly into the liturgy.

It is not intended that the liturgy should stop at these problems; rather, starting from them the text and context of the liturgy should enable Christians (and catechumens) to understand the real meaning of such problems and their significance according to Christian revelation. From such an understanding they should naturally be motivated to relevant action within the context of their daily life and responsibilities. Thus the three aspects of proclaiming the Word of God, celebrating the Word in worship, and witnessing to the Word in service and love can be related to each other in such a manner that each inspires the other. It is their dissociation that often tends to engender Christians who worship in public solemnly but do not witness to

Christian values in ordinary life. The content of preaching is also likely to improve and be more relevant when such themes are consciously and explicitly incorporated within the liturgical cycle.

An Action-Oriented Liturgy

If Christian communities are to participate in the on-going revolutionary struggles for a better world, the liturgy must be related to them. The weekly gatherings for worship are the principal occasions when Christians meet. At present they are geared to action, but this is in connection with church-centered projects: church feasts, devotions, fund-raising for schools and social services, and the work of parish associations. The need is to link more seriously with the efforts of a people for their self-liberation from poverty, oppression, affluence, lack of freedom, and so forth.

One of the difficulties is that the liturgy brings together large numbers, and hence decision-making may be difficult. Here the communications media can help bring issues to the consciousness of the participants. Small-group discussions may be a valuable means of communication and arriving at action. This may be feasible within an hour-long worship period. Those more interested may meet outside the service. Such action does take place when there is an emergency like a flood. The Christian communities have to gear themselves to the worldwide emergency of hunger and famine coupled with exploitation.

The Chinese cultural revolution suggests methods by which large groups could be interested in public service for a cause. China had nationwide campaigns of education and action. The re-education processes were intended to bring about a mental reorientation. Christians, too, need to go through a profound cultural revolution, so that they can be a force opposed to injustice and tyranny wherever they are. The strategies need to be thought over in Christian groups in relation to liturgy, catechesis, and the general life of the community. The weekly meetings of Christians provide a wonderful opportunity for both inner personal growth and social commitment—if they are wisely and courageously utilized. The entire revolution in mass media provides another powerful channel of conscientization.

Recently I participated in a two-hour session on Holy Saturday evening when 150 persons—young and old—had a discussion prior to the solemn Easter Vigil celebration. The assembly began with a discussion in small groups for one hour. The questions were: Why was Jesus killed? How did the early Christians live their understanding of the paschal mystery? How do we now celebrate it in our churches? After this the groups reported their views to the plenary assembly. This was followed by a talk helping to clarify the issues and lead on to further action. As there was much interest in the continuation of this discussion and action, a meeting of those especially interested was fixed for the following Saturday evening.

Such a response was possible because the young enthusiastic parish priest had prepared the people during seven previous Saturdays for a deeper understanding of Jesus and his message. He had been helping the formation of a real community spirit during one and a half years. Thus the parish was attuned to it. The Easter liturgy of the Eucharist was also well participated in. The proclamation of the liberative mission of the Lord in his death-resurrection, presented in popular operatic style, was a highlight of the vigil.

THE EUCHARIST AND A NEW WORLD ORDER

The existing world order, or disorder, is quite contrary to the values of the Eucharist. Whereas the Eucharist is the sacrament of loving sharing, the world system is greedily exploitative. The Eucharist should build community; but world relations are destroying persons and peoples. The Eucharist is universalist; the world is racist. The power of the Eucharist tends toward an egalitarian society; but the world powers are hegemonistic. Whereas the Eucharist motivates humble service, arrogant domination prevails on the international scene. The eucharistic bread is a common meal for all; but bread in the world is a commodity for trade. In the eucharistic ideal, land is for common use; in the present system of nation-states, land is for the successful conquerors. The Eucharist gives a priority to persons; in international relations, power and profit prevail. There is much injustice within countries. But the injustice at the world level is much more tragic. What is worse is that it is precisely those who profess to be Christians who are the main exploiting powers. Those who celebrate the Eucharist are also the chief agents of arms production, selfish profit maximization, ostentatious waste, and land-grabbing. We can thus see the terrible crimes with which the Eucharist has been and is associated historically and today.

Since the Christian churches are quasi-universal in their presence, they have a very grave responsibility toward the correction of these disorders at the world level. They must have effective strategies for bringing about the needed mental and structural changes at the world level. This is particularly urgent because there is as yet no world governmental agency capable of controlling the greed of nation-states. The churches are linked throughout the world. Earlier, they generally had an influence for domesticating peoples within capitalism and imperialism. Now, they can be powerful agents of human liberation—if they really want to be so.

The theology of the Eucharist must become planetary. *We need a global spirituality.* This is not an abstract or distant ideal. The bread used for the Eucharist in Sri Lanka is sometimes from Australia, Canada, or the United States. The wine may be from southern Europe. In a similar vein, when the British people go to Mass on a Sunday they meet persons from several countries. At the same Mass there will be directors and workers from companies like Unilever, Shell, and Nestlé that have bases in about two-thirds of the world. Our daily life is related to different parts of the world. Our meals, our clothes, our transport, all link several peoples of the world. Many of us eat daily bread produced by the sweat of exploited peoples' labor. Since the Eucharist is the sacrament of unity, it must also be the sacrament of world justice.

The meaning of the church as *one*, *universal*, and *Catholic* must be rethought in terms of the planetary oneness of the human family today. The churches can be most significant alliances for liberation if the eucharistic groups across the world are linked to each other. This can take place around issues and action programs. This happens somewhat when there is a natural calamity such as a major earthquake. But there is no similar consciousness of the worldwide continuing calamity of tens of millions dying of hunger. Conscience has not been awakened to these. Where the news media bring us the tales of woe, we have built up our defenses. Patchwork charity is often the furthest we are prepared to go.

The tragedy of the human race is being so rapidly aggravated that eucharistic groups cannot neglect their global responsibility for long without being guilty of reducing religious ceremony to hypocrisy. The opposition to the Vietnam war by the more sensitive United States groups showed the potential of the reflecting eucharistic group to be a catalyst of desirable action even in a big country like the United States. The internationalization of the concern for sharing bread should be one of the directions in which the Eucharist can and must evolve during the coming decades. This in turn will help give meaning to personal life and to community. Christian ecumenism would then be more related to inter-people justice. The prayer of Jesus at the Last Supper "that they may all be one" will then have a more profound significance for our times and problems.

The churches must have a conscious policy for bringing about international sharing on a basis of justice and not charity. The wealth, resources, and land of the world must be for all, and especially for those in need. The sharing of technology cannot be merely on the principle of further profit accumulation for the powerful. The Christian approach to the transfer of technology has to be much more egalitarian than anything that the United Nations Conference on Trade and Development (UNCTAD) or the United Nations itself has so far proposed. The eucharistic relationship to the Jewish Jubilee Year, when lands were returned and debts written off, can be a powerful motivation for a just reconsideration of the growing debt among nations. The common table of the Eucharist, where the same Lord is received all over the world, can be a very strong motivation for approaches like the UNCTAD Common Fund for ensuring a fair deal for the producers of primary commodities.

In its planetary dimension, the theology of the Eucharist is still in its infancy. The churches have to think together collectively, creatively, and relevantly. They can come into this world-wide struggle as a committed ally of the weak. The religious orders and congregations which are international, and which have dedicated persons in many countries at the grassroots level, can be the conveyor belts of such thinking and action. The minimum they could do would be to support the reformist policies of such world bodies as UNCTAD, the International Labour Organisation, the Food and Agriculture Organization, and the World Health Organization. But we need to go much further if we are to respond to the revolutionary demands of the Gospel of Jesus Christ.

The churches must evolve a planetary catechesis to communicate the message of human unity in justice. The pastorate needs strategies of action, transforming the eucharistic groups into a people on the march toward integral liberation. In this, intense struggle and active contestation are inevitable. Risk-bearing would return to the eucharistic table. The cross would be the lot of many believers then. Along with all others who are in the same struggle, Christians then would be crusaders for a more holy cause of making human life worthwhile for all on earth. Today we have the means to do so, but we lack the determination and the political will to live the Gospel in the real world. Eucharistic gatherings would then be among the vanguard of the building of the new world in hard work, real sharing, and justice. As the churches begin to relate to these issues, they will forget their petty concerns with rubrics and ritualism and enter the heart of the human search today. They will then be among the foremost harbingers of the real new international economic order, which has to be a foretaste of the ultimate kingdom of peace and justice promised by God in Jesus Christ.

To the poor man God dare not appear except in the form of bread and the promise of work. Grinding pauperism cannot lead to anything else than moral degradation. Every human being has a right to live and therefore to find the wherewithal to feed himself.

—*Mahatma Gandhi*

Chapter XI

Liturgy, Cultures, and Religions

In the renewal of the Eucharist and of the entire liturgy, our cultures and religions are of paramount importance. Christianity unfortunately came back to Asia heavily clothed in a dominant foreign garb. The Latin Catholic and Protestant churches were inculturated in Europe. Unlike the oriental churches, they could hardly think of Christianity except through European cultural molds. Among Catholics the control was so rigid that up to some fifteen years ago a priest could not even say "The Lord be with you" (i.e., *Dominus vobiscum*) at Mass in any language other than Latin.

This is contrary to the attitude of the other missionary world religions. Buddhism and Islam have adapted themselves to the cultures of the different Asian countries in which they are spread. These cultures themselves have evolved with the religions. Buddhism is Thai in Thailand, Burman in Burma, and Japanese in Japan. Islam is Indian in India, Pakistani in Pakistan, Indonesian in Indonesia. Catholic and Protestant Christianity, on the other hand, maintained their western forms in all the Asian countries.

The question of culture is not merely one of external forms of expression and presentation. Culture expresses the soul of a people. It is a point of entry into their personalities and societies. It expresses the finer sentiments and deeper feelings of a people. It is the bearer of the values that are treasured by them. In many ways Christians remained marginal to these in Asia.

The liberative message of the Gospel can best be related

to the peoples of Asia and Africa in and through their cultures. These cultures too need to go through a process of purification due to the amalgam of superstition and conservatism that they sometimes bear. In such a cultural reorientation of Christianity, the Eucharist is of great significance. For it is around the Eucharist that a culture expresses itself more articulately in what is specific to the Christians. The eucharistic gathering is central to the life of the Christian community even from a merely sociological perspective. In Sri Lanka we notice that the Portuguese seem to have entered more fully into the culture and social life of the Sinhalese and Tamils than the Dutch. The Portuguese way of life, music, folk dances, and human relations brought them closer to the Sri Lankans than did the way of the rather aloof, matter-of-fact Dutch. This may explain to some extent why Dutch Reformed Protestantism virtually disappeared after the end of Dutch rule, whereas Catholicism survived one and a half centuries of persecution and discrimination.

With the British an effort was made to impose another culture through the intermediary of the Anglicized local elite and the Christian missionaries. This process was countered only after the universal franchise in 1931, political independence in 1948, and especially after the social changes following the 1956 general elections. Measures such as the spread of education to the rural areas, the change in the medium of instruction to Sinhala and Tamil, and making Sinhala the official language (with reasonable use of Tamil) have had a greater impact on the cultural life of the churches in Sri Lanka than any internal rethinking and renewal by Christians themselves. The younger generation of the native clergy are thus more attuned to Sinhala and Tamil than to English or Latin. The stopping of the entry of Catholic foreign missionaries around 1952 also facilitated this adaptation. However, it must be mentioned that there were several European missionaries who knew the local languages better than the earlier generation of English-educated local clergy. Now the push toward the local languages and cultures is much stronger, as almost the whole of the younger generation below about thirty years is more fluent in Sinhala or Tamil than in English. The demand for *Eelan*—a separate state for the Tamils—is likely to be associated with a more conscious revival of Tamil culture in which Hindus, Christians, and Muslims will be associated.

The Constitution on the Liturgy lays down a clear policy:

> Even in the liturgy, the Church has no wish to impose a rigid uniformity in matters which do not implicate the faith or the good of the whole community; rather does she respect and foster the genius and the talents of the various races and peoples.
>
> Anything in these peoples' way of life which is not indissolubly bound up with superstition and error, she studies with sympathy, and, if possible, preserves intact. Sometimes, in fact, she admits such things into the liturgy itself so long as they harmonize with its true and authentic spirit (no. 37).

Theoretically this policy has been accepted; in fact it has been so for quite some time, even prior to the council. Yet its practical implementation is still restricted in most of Asia. A major obstacle to liturgical reform in this direction is the way Christians, including priests and bishops, in Asia have been brought up. Owing to a strictly disciplined formation, which regarded uniformity as almost an ultimate value, and due also to a disregard of ancient cultures even by native Christians, it has not been easy to carry out the reform and "adaptation" desired by the council.

LITURGY AND CULTURES

For the purposes of discussion it is useful to distinguish between what is merely of the culture of a country and what belongs to the other religions. The cultural elements can be considered for incorporation in the liturgy without any serious theological difficulties; a problem here would be the trends of evolution of Asian cultures under the impact of modernization.

Among the main cultural elements may be placed some

rites, such as for marriages and funerals, and certain festivities. At present some of these festivities, such as the
New Year and the Feast of Lights, are celebrated mainly
by those of other religions. For example, in most Southeast
Asian countries New Year celebrations occur somewhere
between February and April. In certain countries, like
Thailand and Cambodia, Christians observe these ceremonies. Yet in other places like Sri Lanka Christians are
by and large not involved. The commemoration of ancestors in countries like Vietnam, China, and Japan may also
be regarded as an event of cultural interest, even though it
may have a religious aspect. It is somewhat similar to the
celebration of national heroes' days.

We have to seek the values signified and realized by
these festivities and try to participate in their promotion.
New Year's Day, for instance, is an occasion for a renewal
of family ties, for filial homage to parents and for friendly
visits to relatives and neighbors. Yet in some countries
these have been given up by Christians because the festivities were considered to be "pagan" practices. *Dee-
pavali*, the Feast of Lights, could help us to reflect on the
enlightenment of persons. The trends in these directions
are still too slow and hesitant.

Another characteristic of the oriental cultures is their
emphasis on simplicity, especially in relation to religious
services. People going to temples wear simple white dress
without any signs of distinction. Christians go to worship
in their "Sunday best." The church tends to be a place for
fashion trend-setting and ostentation. This too gives the
Christian community an impression of being an alienated
group in the Asian setting. Greater simplicity in dress and
lifestyle can help in the cultural integration of Christians.

The whole field of art, theater, music, and dancing offers
a wide area of renewal and inculturation for the Christian
liturgy in Asia and Africa. Naturally this requires a liberation from the rather rigid type of ceremony to which the
Roman liturgy is accustomed. The cultural traditions of
the peoples of Asia and Africa have accustomed them to

discussion within groups, as a family, a village, or a tribe. The needs of gearing the liturgy to personal and group action-reflection can benefit from such customs. Mao Tse-tung's China has utilized such means in the running of communes and in linking up the whole people for their mass campaigns.

In the cultural adaptation of the Eucharist we should consider to what extent the use of bread and wine are absolutely essential in our context. Bread is not the daily food of most Asians, and certainly not the unleavened bread in the form of hosts. Alcoholic drinks, including wines, are not the habitual drink in Asian countries, as they are in the Mediterranean region. The Asian religions do not favor the use of alcoholic liquors. Often wine has to be imported from the temperate zones. How far can the eucharistic practices change in this regard? Would not some other forms of food and drink be more acceptable? This is not a major issue now; but some consideration should be given to it. A change or flexibility in this could increase the meaningfulness of the Eucharist.

The cultural renewal of the liturgy will also have to respond to the growing new culture of the cities, especially among the youth. We have seen earlier how the values of the youth in our countries have much in common with the youth in the rest of the world. A secular culture is evolving in which the accents are more on freedom and self-realization. Sometimes Asian youth find that the earlier cultural patterns of their own societies cramp initiative and alienate them from their values and aspirations.

The reorientation of culture in relation to the liturgy has also to respond to the needs of the entire liberative struggle in society. Human liberation will not be achieved without combating internal and external obstacles to it. The liturgy can make an important contribution to such a task. For this there has to be a transformation of culture to contest the evils of selfishness within us and in the structures of society. In some way the element of contesting such evils has to come into the liturgy. The catacombs of old, where the liturgy was also celebrated, were a sort of "underground" of passive resistance of the claims of the emperors to divinity and absolute power. With the spread of dictatorship in many Afro-Asian countries, the liturgy is becoming in some way a place of counterculture. The Eucharist as a motivation for sharing can find itself in conflict with the growing inequalities of a capitalist society or the imbalances in power under a Marxist dictatorship. All these indicate that a pluriformity of cultural approaches is required for responding to the demands of the rapidly evolving Afro-Asian countries.

LITURGY AND THE OTHER RELIGIONS OF ASIA

Since the human search for fulfillment is universal, those who profess different religions should learn to appreciate and respect the believers in religions other than theirs. Christians have much to regret and much to learn in this respect. We have tried to give some indications of how the liturgy can help in this. This is a difficult task due to the differences in language and sensitivities. What we write here is naturally from a Christian point of view and has to be understood from that perspective.

While Christianity teaches respect for all persons and greater respect to those who are the great teachers and spiritual leaders of humankind, we must sincerely admit that over the past generations, Christianity in Ceylon has not been formed in this spirit. In fact in the past, Sinhalese —not to mention the foreign rulers—conceived of Christianity as being in opposition to the religion preached by the Buddha. The events of those centuries have left unpleasant memories in the historical consciousness of the Buddhist people of this country.

Attitude Toward Other Religions

We are fortunate that at last in our generation we can try to undo the damage of such unfortunate relationships by more humane and more authentically spiritual approaches. Naturally in the process of building understanding among religious groups we should neither dilute our faith nor be opportunistic in our attitudes toward persons of other religions. Christians of today have the advantage of our times—to be able to recognize better the fact and the value of the plurality of religions in the country and the world.

Christians now have a greater realization of the immense spiritual treasures of the great world religions. They recognize that all these religions share in some way in the truth about ultimate human destiny and happiness both here and hereafter. We have come to see better that truth can have many aspects and be understood by different peoples in different ways—even though the truth in itself is one.

For Catholics Vatican II has consolidated these gains succinctly in the Declaration on the Relation of the Church to Non-Christian Religions:

> Thus *in Hinduism,* men contemplate the divine mystery and express it through an inexhaustible abundance of myths and through searching philosophical inquiry. They seek freedom from the anguish of our human condition either through ascetical practices or profound meditation or a flight to God with love and trust.
>
> Again, *Buddhism,* in its various forms, realizes the radical insufficiency of this changeable world: it teaches a way by which men, in a devout and confident spirit, may be able either to acquire the state of perfect liberation, or attain, by their own efforts or through higher help, supreme illumination. Likewise, other religions found everywhere try to counter the restlessness of the human heart, each in its own manner, by proposing "ways," comprising teachings, rules of life, and sacred rites. . . .
>
> The Church regards with esteem also the *Moslems.* They adore the one God, living and subsisting in Himself, merciful and all powerful, the Creator of heaven and earth, who has spoken to men; they take pains to submit wholeheartedly to even His inscrutable decrees, just as Abraham, with whom the faith of Islam takes pleasure in linking itself, submitted to God. Though they do not acknowledge Jesus as God, they revere him as a prophet.

They also honor Mary, his virgin mother; at times they even call on her with devotion. In addition, they await the day of judgment when God will render their deserts to all those who have been raised up from the dead. Finally, they value the moral life and worship God especially through prayer, almsgiving and fasting.

Since in the course of centuries not a few quarrels and hostilities have arisen between Christians and Moslems, this Sacred Synod urges all to forget the past and to work sincerely for mutual understanding and to preserve as well as to promote together for the benefit of all mankind social justice and moral welfare, as well as peace and freedom.

The Catholic Church rejects nothing that is true and holy in these religions. She regards with sincere reverence those ways of conduct and of life, those precepts and teachings which, though differing in many aspects from the ones she holds and sets forth, nonetheless often reflect a ray of that Truth which enlightens all men (nos. 2–3).

The council, while emphasizing the uniqueness of Christ as "the way, the truth, and the life," exhorts Christians to promote the values of the other religions:

The Church, therefore, exhorts her sons, that through dialogue and collaboration with the followers of other religions, carried out with prudence and love and in witness to the Christian faith and life, they recognize, preserve and promote the good things, spiritual and moral, as well as the socio-cultural values formed among these men (no. 2).

The Decree on Missionary Activity relates the mission of the church to the fulfillment of what is good in other religions.

Hence, whatever elements of good are found in the minds and hearts of men, or sown among the rites and cultures of various people, far from being lost, they are corrected and elevated, and thus contribute to the glory of God, the confusion of the devil and the happiness of man (no. 9).

It is part of the mission of the church to recognize the

values in other religions; for us these ultimately are of God and it is through them that the fullness of Christ can be realized on earth.

We cannot dialogue in any depth with persons of other religions while abstracting from their allegiance to those religions. We cannot understand these persons, their cultures, and their countries if we do not try to understand and appreciate the religions themselves, and not merely the religions as such but also the persons who have been leading lights of these religions. We cannot truly understand and appreciate Buddhists if we do not try to understand and appreciate Buddhism and especially Gautama the Buddha himself. We must therefore have a satisfactory view of the role of the Buddha in our world vision and in our Christian thinking.

A method of Christian witness can be: acceptance of such values; incorporation of these within our own way of life—a certain incarnation; witness to the specific Christian message and reality with reference to these values. This process involves a transformation or breakaway from what is not good in any human traditions and situations.

Such an approach implies an acceptance of the presence of Christ in those outside the visible dimension of the Christian church. From this acceptance it is our mission to witness to the role of Christ in human history and within persons. The acceptance of other religions can include the acceptance of their values and some of their rites and symbolism without, however, accepting superstitious elements. From this we may consider the acceptance of the great religious leaders as well. Let us, however, proceed step by step, in order to keep the issues clear and to permit any to agree with whatever they might like without feeling obliged thereby to accept everything said here.

Acceptance of Values of Other Religions

The stage seems to be set now for moving from an irenic attitude to one of greater communion in the values of other religions. It would have been difficult to say this decades ago without being in some way offensive to the "pious" sentiments of Christians. But as the relationships among the religions improve, we begin to see that there are many positive values in all religions. It must be our task to discover and discern these values and, where feasible, incorporate them even within our liturgy.

Some such values may be mentioned here by way of example. Buddhism lays great stress on meditation. In more refined forms its religious practices emphasize the effort of self-purification through reflection. In Buddhism there is an effort at auto-liberation from the sorrowful cycle of birth and death. All countries in which Buddhism has had a deep impact are marked by this approach: Burma, Thailand, Japan, China, Cambodia, and Sri Lanka. The liturgy can benefit much from a consideration of the importance of quiet reflection. In sacramental ministrations we could accentuate more the necessity of a personal response by the recipients—the *ex opere operantis* aspect.

Similar suggestions may be made concerning other values, such as detachment, unselfishness in thought and action, the spirit of selfless service, fasting, simplicity of life, temperance, and resignation. It is true that Christianity acknowledges these values. But in an Asian context we can begin by appreciating the values in others, making them our own insofar as they are good, and thereafter communicating whatever is specific in the Christian revelation concerning them. This would be the proper catechetical method; it could also be the acceptable approach in the liturgy so that we can begin with values and even texts which are known and understood by the entire people. It would thus enable the liturgy really to communicate meaning even to followers of other religions who have occasion to attend our ceremonies, such as weddings and funerals.

In order to promote spiritual values in all as exhorted by Vatican Council II, we must first know and appreciate the spiritual values in others and in other religions. These religions, too, have certain occasions when the values are recalled, rekindled, and heightened. In Sri Lanka, *Vesak* is pre-eminently such an event; it is the festivity that has the greatest impact on persons and on the life of the community. Vesak is a memorial to the life and message of the Buddha and a time for the renewal of the moral conscience of his followers, who form over two-thirds of Sri Lanka's inhabitants.

Vesak is an event that brings to the surface many of the virtues that characterize the life of the good Buddhist. We must therefore be happy that Buddhists insist on the spiritual significance of Vesak: for example on *sil*, on meditation and self-abnegation, on almsgiving and loving-kindness. On that day hundreds of thousands remind themselves of the path of selfless service that Buddhism inculcates. Friendliness abounds and finds practical expression in the thousands of *dansalas* where everyone who passes by is invited to a communion in partaking of the food given by the community of the area. The *dansala* is a symbol of *metta* (loving-kindness as an active force) that goes out in *karuna* (compassion, identification with the other in need) to welcome and refresh pilgrims and travelers.

Vesak is also a great feast of light and joy—the sympathetic joy in thankfulness for the light of the Buddha. It is a joy that is unselfish and is the opposite of envy. Love and joy find their expression in the festivity and the Vesak lanterns which proclaim to the world that on that day a luminous message of liberation from the tragic condition of human existence has been announced to humankind. The Vesak pavilions around which multitudes throng are a form of religious instruction of the masses; the stories from the life of the Buddha and the history of Buddhism are thus explained to them.

Are not all these spiritual values about which we can be happy and which we can ourselves promote? To honor the Buddha is not to undervalue Christ, for it is part of Christ's teaching that "where there is love and charity, there God is." In fact the only way to spread love and charity is by appreciating others at the deepest and noblest level of their being; we shall then merit for ourselves a similar understanding. We must frankly reassess our attitudes. It will be a happy day in our land, when without fear or scandal we Christians, too, join Buddhists in honoring the memory of one who has really been a light of the East.

Rites and Symbolism of Other Religions

Liturgical rites and symbolism have to be revised in order that they may be meaningful for the people of our times and our countries. The Council Fathers were agreed on this principle. One line of reform is to make them relevant to our modern technological world with its secular preoccupations; another is to render them intelligible to the different peoples of the world according to their sociocultural and religious traditions. The Roman liturgy evolved according to the cultural traditions of the Latins. In the rites we can distinguish elements which are from Jesus and may therefore be immutable and of universal value, and other elements which are of church origin and hence can be changed.

The rites in Asian countries for ceremonies such as marriages, funerals, and other events of social significance are often different from those in western countries. Vatican Council II has already advocated and permitted the revision of liturgical rites. The Constitution on the Sacred Liturgy states:

The marriage rite now found in the Roman Ritual is to be revised and enriched in such a way that the grace and the sacrament are more clearly signified and the duties of the spouses are taught.

If any regions are wont to use other praiseworthy customs and ceremonies when celebrating the sacrament of matrimony, the sacred Synod earnestly desires that these by all means be retained.

Moreover the competent territorial ecclesiastical authority mentioned in art. 22 of this Constitution is free to draw up its own rite suited to the usage of place and people, according to the provision of art. 63 (no. 77).

Even the Council of Trent provided for this adaptation over four hundred years ago; yet few Asian countries seem to have so far availed themselves of this opportunity. It is now most opportune and important that liturgical rites be revised accordingly. In some countries, such as Vietnam and China, other feasts and rites, like those connected with the cult of ancestors, could be somewhat integrated within the Catholic liturgy.

The symbolism of the rites of the other religions—such as ablutions, lights, simple white dress, flowers—are often more connected with the socio-cultural milieu than specifically with religious beliefs. They are media that communicate well to our peoples and could be incorporated into the Christian liturgy.

It is of course understood that what is mere superstition should not be taken over; but even the other religious leaders do not approve of that.

Acceptance of the Sacred Writings of Asia

In dialogue with peoples of the world Asians must acknowledge the influence of their great leaders, especially in the religious sphere. The Scriptures, including the New Testament writings, contain quotations from the writings of believers in other religions of the times in which they were written.

There is a great wealth of spiritual writings in the East. They are part of the original "revelation" of God to humankind in these countries, however veiled this revelation might be. It is works like the Vedas, the Dhammapada, and the teachings of Confucius and Lao-tse which have nourished the soul of Asians for countless generations. They have a power of captivating the Asian people. Asians can accept and incorporate what is good in these teachings into their teaching of religion—catechesis—and also their meditation and worship.

The reform of the liturgy of the Word offers excellent

opportunities for this approach, which also seems indicated by missiological perspectives. The liturgy of the Word, even in the Mass, can be revised to include more relevant readings from these Scriptures. Would it not be possible for passages from the sacred writings of the East to be included in the readings for the Divine Office and in the service of the Word which was the Mass of the catechumens?

Such an approach would provide continuity from the other religions to Christianity and its liturgy. Catechumens and converts would feel more at ease in the Christian community. Christians, including the clergy and the religious, would be more integrated into the sacred tradition of their own culture and country. This would not mean a neglect of the essential values of Christianity; on the contrary, they would be seen in the context of God's revelation to others. The Christian Scriptures and the core of the eucharistic liturgy would constantly bear witness to them.

Respect for the Spiritual Leaders of Asia

From a consideration of cultures, values, rites, symbolism, and writings we can move on to ask what respect could be given to the great spiritual leaders of Asia, like the Buddha, Mohammed, and Confucius, in the thinking and even the liturgy of the Christians.

Most great spiritual leaders are from Asia. It is our duty to respect and reverence those who have done good to us. These leaders, especially the Buddha, have contributed more to the spiritual formation of the peoples of Asian countries than any saints of the Christian religion. Their teaching does not contain the total revelation in Jesus Christ; but we can regard their deep spiritual insights and influence as a grace of God to us. Hence when we honor them we honor the gifts of God in Christ and the Holy Spirit as received and fructified in them. To honor them is also a way of witnessing to our good will and concern for the many who reverence them. Whether we appreciate it or not, Asian civilization has been shaped by them.

There may be a certain fear in honoring them insofar as

less well-informed Christians might think that either we give them the honor due to God or that we accept everything they teach as the truth. But even the followers of these religions do not regard the Buddha, Confucius, Mohammed, or Gandhi as God, in the sense in which we speak of God. Whatever it be, this danger of a certain amount of scandal must be weighed against our obligation to give honor where it is due and against the scandal given to those who are not Christians by our reluctance to recognize goodness outside our fold.

If it is agreed that we could honor these leaders, how could we do so and what relationship could this have to our liturgy? This is, quite understandably, an area where difference of opinion is possible and likely; and any objection to what follows need not necessarily prejudice the earlier recommendations. It seems to us that we—especially Asians—could celebrate certain festivities in honor of these great saintly leaders of humanity. We could, for instance, venerate the Buddha on Vesak day when his birth, enlightenment, and death are commemorated. How could we do so? Could we not join with the followers of the Buddha in meditation as well as public rejoicing and happiness?

Further, could we not, even within the context of our liturgy, celebrate their virtues and their virtuous doctrines which are from God? Could we not be thankful collectively and in public for the signal graces of the spiritual leadership of these gurus? Do their lives not have a relationship to the paschal mystery? Such an approach would open to us greater possibilities of interreligious cooperation. More good will be generated; and others will see the true universality of Christianity, which has to welcome what is good, not destroy it.

Interreligious Action-Reflection

The radical transformation of the world and of the mentalities of people is not likely to come about without the participation and cooperation of believers in the world religions. In such action an ongoing reflection in groups both big and small is an essential element. No deep cultural revolution is possible without a profound reflection that changes values. Such a reflection can be made on the inspiration of the Christian Scriptures in the western countries including Latin America, and perhaps in the Philippines. But in most countries of Asia and Africa Christians are intermingled with others, who sometimes are the vast majority. If we accept only the Christian Scriptures as the motivation and content of reflection (in addition to the social situation) then the groups that meet will have only Christians.

Action in society generally takes place within groups that have Christians and others. Hence reflection also should make provision for them; otherwise both action and reflection are weakened, and the cause itself impeded. Hence we need in Asia and Africa action-reflection in interreligious groups. This is one of the inadequacies of the exclusively Christian movements, many of which are imported from the West—for example, lay apostolate movements, charismatic prayer groups, even the Latin American emphasis on Christianity in their theology of the praxis of liberation.

If we reflect with believers of other religions we must naturally respect and reflect on their Scriptures too. We can come to a common prayer too. This requires an emphasis on the universal and common aspects of all the great religions. For God is one; or we can be agreed on certain basic ultimate values. This challenge is even greater when we form action groups with humanists, socialists, and Marxists. In these situations, too, it is the search for common values and the sacrifice for a cause that builds the groups. The theology of the cosmic Christ and the indwelling of the Spirit in all are of immediate significance in such situations. Thus a planetary approach to prayer itself is closely related to the universal cooperation required for a global revolutionary strategy. Far too often Christians do not respect enough the honest search and self-sacrifice of many of other faiths and ideologies in the cause of human liberation and hence of the kingdom of God. Frequently it is such persons who lead in these struggles, whereas Christians tend to exhibit a more complacent attitude. In the coming decade this dimension of interreligious reflection and worship needs to be developed. After all, the walls of churches, mosques, temples, kovils, lodges, and synagogues do not reach up to heaven— fortunately.

The contemplatives in the different religious traditions can contribute toward the growth of such forms of reflective worship. Even if they are largely divorced from action, they can study the Scriptures and spirituality of the different religions. They can try to see the common elements and the riches of the diversity. Thomas Merton considered this an important mission of contemplatives—especially in the last stages of his life. His visit to Sri Lanka prior to his final arrival in Bangkok was linked to this quest. His last conference on the role of the monk in a revolutionary world is full of such insights on the interrelation between religious revolutionaries, world justice, and the worship of the Lord. It is to be hoped that the thousands of contemplatives in the Christian tradition will take up this contemporary challenge of the love of God who so loved the world as to give his only son. Contemplation can be a help to building the wider human unity on a spiritual basis of a deeper understanding of the human person, of nature, and of God.

The modern world demonstrates that such intercommunion and deeper spiritual experience is possible at a global level. The universal attraction of the great works of art are an evidence of this. The depth of realism and emotion in the films of great artists like Satyajit Ray and Ingmar Bergman touch the core of the inner being of those who enter into their experience. The world of mass media and art can teach religions something of the basic commonality of the passions, emotions, aspirations, and hopes of every human person.

Appreciating Mystical Experience

Mystical experience is the deepest intuition of the divine that human beings have described. All the great religions have at their heart such a deep experience. The Buddha was a profound mystic; so were the great leaders of the other religions throughout the ages. Islam, Hinduism, and Confucianism have their great spiritual heights. These are the high-watermarks of a human union with God in worship—a worship often linked to action. The Christian spiritual tradition has to recognize and respect the mysticism of all the different traditions. At this level, theologies and definitions of faith do not count so much as the quasi-immediate experience of the Absolute. Even ordinary human beings can have a perception of this inner union within themselves at certain moments of their lives. This is the substance of our relationship to God, the Absolute, and ultimate values. It is where our authenticity is tested at the bar of conscience. The descriptions of the intuition of the Absolute by the great mystics of different religious traditions have much in common. This shows how much less important are the differences of religion than the oneness of humanity in relation to the Absolute. Christians can learn from these experiences of mysticism to respect different forms of worship. They can help evolve forms of common prayer and meditation that can enable persons of different traditions to worship together and commune together with and in the Absolute. Perhaps the more spontaneous prayer groups that are proliferating at the margin of the churches may open themselves to this dimension and reach out to the prayerfulness of believers of other religions.

Nor should we exclude in this consideration the finer sentiments of those of the revolutionary traditions and of the humanists. Great scientists or artists have an element of the mystic in them. A Lenin or a Mao Tse-tung cannot be appreciated without seeing the mystical traits of their struggles and their character. The classless, stateless society of Karl Marx and Friedrich Engels has reminded Christians of their long-forgotten apocalyptic vision and vocation. The lifestyle of Ho Chi Minh has an attractive simplicity and daring that resemble those of the great religious liberators. Humanity will be the richer if as a whole we can come to appreciate such great peaks of human endeavor when they touch something of the divine, consciously or unconsciously. The grace of the Christian can be to recognize them and praise God for his marvels among us.

A Foretaste of the Heavenly Liturgy

The Constitution on the Liturgy reminds us of the eschatological dimension of our liturgy, which seeks to build up the full realization of the kingdom of God. The liturgy helps to realize and manifest this objective.

"In the earthly liturgy we receive a foretaste of that heavenly liturgy which is celebrated in the holy city of Jerusalem towards which we journey as pilgrims . . ." (no. 8).

In the heavenly liturgy all people of good will take part. There are no distinctions of the visible and the invisible church in heaven; all participate in singing "a hymn to the Lord's glory." We must try, within limits, to realize here on earth the universal dimensions of the one liturgy while maintaining its oneness in Christ Jesus. Our view is that all praise God, in and through Jesus Christ, the unique mediator for all humankind. Some know and acknowledge him, others do not even know him. We know that he is at work in all, and that all really honor God by their good lives. Should we not try to bring together as many of these as possible in a universal harmony and justice on earth? Such an integral liberation would be the best contribution of all religions together to humanity.

A Challenge from an Asian Sage

THE HIDDEN GOD

Leave this chanting and singing and telling of beads.

Whom do you worship in this lonely dark corner of the temple with all the doors shut?

Open your eyes and see that God is not in front of you.

He is there where the farmer is tilling the hard ground and where the labourer is breaking stones.

He is with them in the sun and the rain and his garment is covered with dust.

Put off your holy cloak and like him come down on to the dusty soil.

Deliverance?

Where will you find deliverance?

Our master himself has joyfully taken on the bonds of creation; he is bound with us for ever.

Come out of your meditations and leave aside the flowers and the incense;

What harm is there if your clothes become tattered and stained?

Meet him and stand by him in toil and in the sweat of your brow.

—Rabindranath Tagore

Chapter XII

The Radical Mystique
of the Lord's Prayer

Central to the eucharistic celebration is the Lord's Prayer taught by Jesus himself. It is said at every Mass. It was the response of Jesus to the request of one of his disciples, "Lord, teach us to pray." We too can learn from Jesus how to pray. Jesus prayed alone and with others. The Our Father is a prayer that is more communitarian. In the Our Father there are three petitions which are more in relation to God and four others more connected with the human condition. These petitions are found in some form in the Jewish prayers of the period. What Jesus did was to give a new, wider, and deeper content to them. He linked the honoring of God with the concern for neighbor.

"Our Father"

Jesus taught his disciples a new filial way of talking to God. The earlier Jewish prayers spoke to God more as the Creator, King, Lord, and Sovereign Master. Jesus brings in a directness and warmth that characterize his relations with the Father. There is also a childlike simplicity and warmth. He does not encourage long formulae. He assures us that God is a loving father who knows all our needs and cares for every one personally. His revelation is not concerning a God of the philosophers or of infinite overawing majesty. The Father is a God of love.

He says "*Our* Father." Here he does not pray to "my" Father or to the Father of the Jews. God's fatherhood is universal. He makes the sun rise on all, the good and the bad. This goes against any tendency to pray in a mere selfish, individualistic manner to "my God." It also means a rejection of all forms of human discrimination. God is the Father of all humanity: of men and women, of black and white, rich and poor, Jew and gentile. The Our Father can thus be the basis of a radical universality. It implies a fundamental rejection of racism, sexism, and all forms of superiority-consciousness or hatred for others. We are all one under the fatherhood of God. The words "Our Father" give us the sum and substance of the Gospel of Jesus Christ. They teach us the loving universal fatherhood of God and the fellowship of humanity. They bring a tenderness and depth to our relations with both God and other persons. No mere rational philosophy or social analysis ever achieves such a depth of meaning and motivation for radical commitment to human fulfillment.

"Hallowed be thy name"

May God's holiness be recognized more and more by us. God is holiness itself. His holiness is his righteousness, his justice, his love. We need to know this more and more. In the Old Testament there is a gradual revelation of his concern for humanity. He is against all forms of oppression of the weak and the poor. He identifies with them. He undertakes a liberative action against those who oppress his people. May this be known here on earth.

"Thy kingdom come, thy will be done on earth as in heaven"

This God-centered petition also relates to the realization of the values of the kingdom of God among human beings. It can refer to the final eschatological consummation of all things in God. But it refers more specifically to the acceptance of his values by us, in our hearts and in our communities. Here again the prayer concerns an earthly reality: that these values revealed in Jesus may be acknowledged here on earth. They already are the very inspiration of the heavenly relationships. The prayer "thy kingdom come" is a deep call to a radical transformation of ourselves, by a rejection of selfishness.

It is not a sort of magic or nostrum. It is an invitation to action in real life inspired by God's vision for humanity. It requires a purification within ourselves, in the deepest recesses of our being up to the ultimate limits of human possibility. Likewise it postulates radical social changes so that the relationships on earth may be as in heaven. There can then be no exploitation of one person by another, or one group by another. It is in this way that the will of God can be realized on earth. It necessitates a personal ascesis inspired by the highest mystique of deep communion in God our common Father.

Thus even the first three God-centered petitions are related intimately to the condition of human beings on earth. God can be honored by us only as we accept his teachings. We do so when we accept all persons as his children. The love of God and the love of neighbor are equally important. They are one and the same commandment. This is the kernel of the revelation in Jesus Christ. There can be no genuine Christian spirituality that is onesided and thinks that God can be honored or a personality can be developed without direct reference to the rest of the human community. The four human-centered petitions make this even more clear and exacting.

"Give us this day our daily bread"

Having honored the Father and prayed for the acceptance of his vision, Jesus teaches us to pray for our needs. The first priority in this is our food. There are differences of opinion among scholars as to whether this text says "give us today the food we need" or "give us the bread of the following day." But there is agreement that the petition is for the bread that sustains human life. Jesus sees that human beings first need the basic essentials for living: food, clothing, and shelter. The petition is communitarian "give us . . . our" daily bread. It is not an individualistic prayer. It implies concern for others too.

We cannot therefore recite the Our Father honestly if we do not care about food for others. Food cannot be ensured for all persons regularly without sufficient production and satisfactory distribution. These in turn will not be brought about unless the socio-economic and political structures of our societies have a minimum of efficiency and justice. Those who pray the Our Father have to oppose situations where some are selfish and amass wealth while others are impoverished and unable to procure the basic essentials of living. Believers in Christ must then contest the waste of resources, the mass unemployment, and the grave inequalities which characterize the present world system.

There is therefore a *political dimension* in the Lord's Prayer. It demands radical changes within countries and in the whole world. The Our Father calls for *a truly new world order* in which the basic needs of all humanity are provided for and all the resources of the earth, including land, are equitably shared. It is indeed a strange irony that among the poor countries of the world it is principally in the socialist and Marxist-ruled areas that food, clothing, housing, and employment are effective. On the other hand, it is the peoples who are the chief agents of world exploitation who also recite the Our Father most often.

The Our Father is a radical rejection of all systems of selfish competition and arms stockpiling. It requires of us a resistance to situations of hunger and malnutrition in which many children die because they lack food and drugs while others spend their lives in wasteful luxury.

"Forgive us our sins as we forgive others"

It is significant that Jesus makes our forgiving of others the condition of our own forgiveness by God. This too brings a communitarian and human dimension to our relationship with God. A readiness to forgive all and fully from our hearts is made a highest priority. Mercy and reconciliation are incumbent on the follower of Jesus. Hatred, envy, and jealousy can have no place in one's heart. This requires a preparedness to be deeply unselfish. In it the community of persons is implied in the heart of our relationships. We cannot be at peace with the Father if we do not have a profound inner peace within ourselves in relation to all other human beings. We are perhaps so accustomed to reciting these words that we do not often realize their radical and mystical dimension. Christians committed to social change have also to nurture a profound love and compassion for all persons. They must contest the evils in society; but inner forgiveness has to temper their relationships. This is a fine combination of revolutionary commitment and love for all. In this sense Jesus is a revolutionary and a lover, a revolutionary because he is a lover. We have to live the dynamic of this tension and fight our battles assiduously for integral human liberation with a profound love for all. Jesus thus gives a new criterion and code of human relations that is both a motivation for commitment and a program of continuing inner personal purification. Forgiveness has to be a liberation of both oppressor and oppressed in a transformed relationship.

"Do not lead us to the test but deliver us from evil"

This is not a prayer to be kept away from trials and difficulties, but rather to be helped in them. We ask the Father to see that we do not succumb to the temptations and difficulties involved in our human condition. It is a prayer similar to that of Jesus in the Garden of Olives. We can so easily succumb to the selfishness of seeking special privileges of all types: of race, creed, color, class, sex, position. We are strongly tempted to seek our own ease and forget the needs of others. We may find it more comfortable to concern ourselves with our own comfort or "personal holiness" and neglect our community responsibility. We find it hard to forgive everyone from the depths of our being. We ask the help of the Father to be delivered from personal and collective evil; from selfishness within us and among us.

All these taken together make the Our Father a profound challenge to our personal and collective lives. It is as radical as it is profound; as universal as it is deep. It is a prayer that must make us at the same time interiorly contemplative and actively committed to human liberation. It is quite contrary to any "spirituality" that would want to take Christians away from the arena of the struggle for justice and righteousness. It rejects mere formalism and ritualism in worship. It places prayer in the very heart of human life, struggles, and relationships. It is a political program that is uncompromising in giving a priority to the urgent human needs of all. It is a challenging approach to human relationships that bears mercy and forgiveness across all frontiers that divide persons and human hearts. It links inextricably the love of God and the concern for others. It is a masterpiece of Jesus' revelation of the fatherhood of God and of human solidarity. It gives the true spirituality of the Eucharist. It explains why Jesus contested all forms of evil prevailing in his day and helped in the integral liberation of persons. That ıs why he was killed. His body and blood were given for others in this cause. It is what he invites us to do when we meet him in the Eucharist. "Do this in commemoration of me."

As you cannot go to heaven alone,
Food is to be shared . . .
As all share the sight of the heavenly stars,
So food is something that must be shared . . .
Ah! food is something that must be shared.

    —*Kim Chi Ha, a Christian,*
    one of Korea's best-known
    poets, from his "Declaration
    of Conscience," smuggled out
    of prison.

Other Orbis books . . .

THE MEANING OF MISSION

José Comblin

"This very readable book has made me think, and I feel it will be useful for anyone dealing with their Christian role of mission and evangelism." *New Review of Books and Religion*
ISBN 0-88344-304-X CIP   *Cloth $6.95*

THE GOSPEL OF PEACE AND JUSTICE

Catholic Social Teaching Since Pope John

Presented by Joseph Gremillion

"Especially valuable as a resource. The book brings together 22 documents containing the developing social teaching of the church from *Mater et Magistra* to Pope Paul's 1975 *Peace Day Message on Reconciliation.* I watched the intellectual excitement of students who used Gremillion's book in a justice and peace course I taught last summer, as they discovered a body of teaching on the issues they had defined as relevant. To read Gremillion's overview and prospectus, a meaty introductory essay of some 140 pages, is to be guided through the sea of social teaching by a remarkably adept navigator."
National Catholic Reporter
"An authoritative guide and study aid for concerned Catholics and others." *Library Journal*
ISBN 0-88344-165-9   *Cloth $15.95*
ISBN 0-88344-166-7   *Paper $8.95*

THEOLOGY IN THE AMERICAS

Papers of the 1975 Detroit Conference

Edited by Sergio Torres and John Eagleson

"A pathbreaking book from and about a pathbreaking theological conference, *Theology in the Americas* makes a major contribution to ecumenical theology, Christian social ethics and liberation movements in dialogue." *Fellowship*
ISBN 0-88344-479-8 CIP   *Cloth $12.95*
ISBN 0-88344-476-3   *Paper $5.95*

CHRISTIANS, POLITICS
AND VIOLENT REVOLUTION

J.G. Davies

"Davies argues that violence and revolution are on the agenda the world presents to the Church and that consequently the Church must reflect on such problems. This is a first-rate presentation, with Davies examining the question from every conceivable angle."

National Catholic News Service

ISBN 0-88344-061-X   *Paper $4.95*

CHRISTIAN POLITICAL THEOLOGY
A MARXIAN GUIDE

Joseph Petulla

"Petulla presents a fresh look at Marxian thought for the benefit of Catholic theologians in the light of the interest in this subject which was spurred by Vatican II, which saw the need for new relationships with men of all political positions." *Journal of Economic Literature*

ISBN 0-88344-060-1   *Paper $4.95*

THE NEW CREATION:
MARXIST AND CHRISTIAN?

José María González-Ruiz

"A worthy book for lively discussion."

The New Review of Books and Religion

ISBN 0-88344-327-9 CIP   *Cloth $6.95*

CHRISTIANS AND SOCIALISM

Documentation of the Christians for
Socialism Movement in Latin America

Edited by John Eagleson

"Compelling in its clear presentation of the issue of Christian commitment in a revolutionary world." *The Review of Books and Religion*

ISBN 0-88344-058-X   *Paper $4.95*

THE CHURCH AND
THIRD WORLD REVOLUTION

Pierre Bigo

"Heavily documented, provocative yet reasonable, this is a testament, demanding but impressive." *Publishers Weekly*

ISBN 0-88344-071-7 CIP   *Cloth $8.95*
ISBN 0-88344-072-5   *Paper $4.95*

WHY IS THE THIRD WORLD POOR?

Piero Gheddo

"An excellent handbook on the Christian understanding of the development process. Gheddo looks at both the internal and external causes of underdevelopment and how Christians can involve themselves in helping the third world." *Provident Book Finder*

ISBN 0-88344-757-6   *Paper $4.95*

POLITICS AND SOCIETY
IN THE THIRD WORLD

Jean-Yves Calvez

"This frank treatment of economic and cultural problems in developing nations suggests the need for constant multiple attacks on the many fronts that produce problems in the human situation."

The Christian Century
ISBN 0-88344-389-9   *Cloth $6.95*

A THEOLOGY OF LIBERATION

Gustavo Gutiérrez

"The movement's most influential text." *Time*

"The most complete presentation thus far available to English readers of the provocative theology emerging from the Latin American Church." *Theological Studies*

"North Americans as well as Latin Americans will find so many challenges and daring insights that they will, I suggest, rate this book one of the best of its kind ever written." *America*

ISBN 0-88344-477-1   *Cloth $7.95*
ISBN 0-88344-478-X   *Paper $4.95*

MARX AND THE BIBLE

José Miranda

"An inescapable book which raises more questions than it answers, which will satisfy few of us, but will not let us rest easily again. It is an attempt to utilize the best tradition of Scripture scholarship to understand the text when it is set in a context of human need and misery."

Walter Brueggemann, in Interpretation

ISBN 0-88344-306-6   *Cloth $8.95*
ISBN 0-88344-307-4   *Paper $4.95*

BEING AND THE MESSIAH

The Message of Saint John

José Miranda

"This book could become the catalyst of a new debate on the Fourth Gospel. Johannine scholarship will hotly debate the 'terrifyingly revolutionary thesis that this world of contempt and oppression can be changed into a world of complete selflessness and unrestricted mutual assistance.' Cast in the framework of an analysis of contemporary philosophy, the volume will prove a classic of Latin American theology." *Frederick Herzog, Duke University Divinity School*

ISBN 0-88344-027-X CIP   *Cloth $8.95*
ISBN 0-88344-028-8   *Paper $4.95*

THE GOSPEL IN SOLENTINAME

Ernesto Cardenal

"Upon reading this book, I want to do so many things—burn all my other books which at best seem like hay, soggy with mildew. I now know who (not what) is the church and how to celebrate church in the eucharist. The dialogues are intense, profound, radical. *The Gospel in Solentiname* calls us home."

Carroll Stuhlmueller, National Catholic Reporter

ISBN 0-88344-168-3   *Vol. 1 Cloth $6.95*
ISBN 0-88344-170-5   *Vol. 1 Paper $4.95*
ISBN 0-88344-167-5   *Vol. 2 Cloth $6.95*

THE CHURCH AND POWER IN BRAZIL
Charles Antoine

"This is a book which should serve as a basis of discussion and further study by all who are interested in the relationship of the Church to contemporary governments, and all who believe that the Church has a vital role to play in the quest for social justice." *Worldmission*
ISBN 0-88344-062-8   *Paper $4.95*

HISTORY AND
THE THEOLOGY OF LIBERATION
Enrique Dussel

"The book is easy reading. It is a brilliant study of what may well be or should be the future course of theological methodology."
Religious Media Today
ISBN 0-88344-179-9   *Cloth $8.95*
ISBN 0-88344-180-2   *Paper $4.95*

DOM HELDER CAMARA
José de Broucker

"De Broucker, an internationally recognized journalist, develops a portrait, at once intimate, comprehensive and sympathetic, of the Archbishop of Olinda and Recife, Brazil, whose championship of political and economic justice for the hungry, unorganized masses of his country and all Latin America has aroused world attention."
America
ISBN 0-88344-099-7   *Cloth $6.95*

THE DESERT IS FERTILE
Dom Helder Camara

"Camara's brief essays and poems are arresting for their simplicity and depth of vision, and are encouraging because of the realistic yet quietly hopeful tone with which they argue for sustained action toward global justice." *Commonweal*
ISBN 0-88344-078-4   *Cloth $3.95*

THEOLOGY FOR A NOMAD CHURCH

Hugo Assmann

"A new challenge to contemporary theology which attempts to show that the theology of liberation is not just a fad, but a new political dimension which touches every aspect of Christian existence."
Publishers Weekly

ISBN 0-88344-493-3   *Cloth $7.95*
ISBN 0-88344-494-1   *Paper $4.95*

FREEDOM MADE FLESH
The Mission of Christ and His Church

Ignacio Ellacuría

"Ellacuría's main thesis is that God's saving message and revelation are historical, that is, that the proclamation of the gospel message must possess the same historical character that revelation and salvation history do and that, for this reason, it must be carried out in history and in a historical way." *Cross and Crown*

ISBN 0-88344-140-3   *Cloth $8.95*
ISBN 0-88344-141-1   *Paper $4.95*

THE LIBERATION OF THEOLOGY

Juan Luis Segundo

"It is a remarkable book in terms of its boldness in confronting the shortcomings of the Christian tradition and in terms of the clarity of vision provided by the hermeneutic of liberation. Segundo writes with ease whether dealing with the sociological, theological, or political roots of liberation. His is a significant addition to the recent work of Cone, Alves, Moltmann, and Gutiérrez because it compels the movement to interrogate its own theological foundations. A necessary addition, in one of the more fruitful directions of contemporary theology, it is appropriate for graduate, undergraduate, or clerical readers." *Choice*

"The book makes for exciting reading and should not be missing in any theological library." *Library Journal*

ISBN 0-88344-285-X CIP   *Cloth $10.95*
ISBN 0-88344-286-8   *Paper $6.95*